Praises "From Simms to

Your book has arrived! Great stuff, packed with wit and wisdom as I knew it would be.

—Baroness Denise Kingsmill,
CBE (Commander of the Most Excellent Order
of the British Empire)

McLeod's life has been truly difficult, but she has managed to pick herself up and do exceedingly well. What's striking about her book is its distinct lack of self-pity: she simply picks herself up when life knocks her down, and gets on with it. The book is full of some practical advice, and it should find McLeod a great many readers.

—19th Annual Writer's Digest
Self-Published Book Awards

Your book could influence the lives of many young people who have their own struggles, and show them that it does get better. All they have to do is keep moving forward, and not wait for their lives to start.

—Auttumn Collins
2012 Valedictorian of James Bowie High School
Simms, Texas

From Simms to Zanzibar will forever be your "wise old friend." Keep it handy, you will want to reread it down the road. Give a copy to those you love. They will be forever grateful. It made me laugh, cry, reflect, wish I'd had this wisdom when I was younger, and showed me the way to live more authentically even now in my fifties. Thank you, Lynn. Your book has renewed my faith in the idea that the written word on "success" can truly be rich and transforming. It's head and shoulders above all the others in this genre. Your writing style made me feel like you were right here at my kitchen table having coffee—laughing, crying and figuring things out –like dear friends do.

—Dr. Debra M. Yoder
Psychology Professor
Mountain View College
Dallas, TX

From Simms to Zanzibar is compact and concise with examples of simple, yet valuable thoughts and truths that in our complex world, we often forget to think about and reflect upon. If students will sit down and read it, they will be able to use it as a tool to help them figure out the paths that they may want to travel and holds many words of inspiration that I hope our kids will take to heart.

I believe that it will be the greatest graduation gift a student could ever get. I found the last two chapters to be very touching, to the point of almost tears.

—Dru Driver
Counselor, James Bowie High School
Simms, TX

From Simms to Zanzibar *took me by surprise, with words of wisdom that accompany a highly motivated and positive attitude … along with a will to succeed. The book is inspiring and thought provoking for any age reader. My 75 years of life experiences pale in comparison to Ms. McLeod's.*

—GayleTP
From Amazon.com review

Every student, every career and every relationship has its ups and downs. From Simms to Zanzibar *is a no-holds-barred journey where author Lynn McLeod is not only your guide, she becomes your coach, confidant and visionary. A terrific read for both enjoyment and solid information in getting to the reader's next step, whatever it may be.*

—Judith Briles
Author, *The Confidence Factor*

Here on the "front lines" of secondary education, I spend my days helping students search for colleges and carve out career paths. Lynn McLeod's experience and advice is priceless to students like mine who need to learn by example about tenacity, motivation and achievement in a world where doing things the easy way is all too common.

—Lisa Albro
Coordinator of College Counseling
Xavier High School
New York, NY

Ms. McLeod's commencement address to the James Bowie Class of 2002 is inspirational not only for its underlying, uplifting themes but its personal message of principled persistence in her lifelong pursuit of self-improvement. The accompanying amplifying material demonstrates that grit, a can-do attitude, and commitment to never, never giving up is a formula that produces success, regardless of circumstances. Her advocating a life of balance is good advice to the new graduate, senior citizen or anyone in between.

—Garey L. McLellan, M.D.
Las Vegas, NV

Lynn McLeod attacks life. She walks in the room, grabs life around the neck, kisses it full on the mouth, and drags it around this old mansion laughing, opening, unlocking, or just kicking in every door she finds. Her story is an inspirational ride that everyone should enjoy.

—Tony Martin
Author, *The Fishkill Mission*

From Simms to Zanzibar

What They Didn't Tell Me
About Success in High School
and I Didn't Know to Ask

Lynn Garrett McLeod

Books may be purchased in quantity and/or special sales
by contacting the publisher:

Zanzibar Press
14405 West Colfax Avenue, Box 189
Golden, CO 80401
www.ZanzibarPress.com

ZANZIBAR PRESS

Cover Design by: NZ Graphics
Layout: WESType Publishing Services, Inc.

Library of Congress Catalog Number: 2010923721

ISBN: 978-0-9844806-1-6

1. Success   2. Teen   3. Motivation   4. Career

10 9 8 7 6 5 4 3

SECOND EDITION, THIRD PRINTING   Printed in Canada

To Mrs. Betty Reed
(1932 to 2009)

She motivated me.

She inspired me.

She believed in me.

Gratitudes and Acknowledgments

There are so many people who have impacted me during my writing journey that it is impossible to name them all—I would have to write another book. If I failed to mention you by name, please forgive me. I will never forget how you, my friends and family, have helped shape my life.

Without the love and protection of my father, grandfather and mother, my life would have taken a different turn, and this book would be far removed from the one you are about to read.

My sister and best friend Debbie (aka Debs): Your love and friendship have sustained me in both good and not-so-good times.

My brother James: You've always been there to walk with me and smooth out the bumps in the road.

Mrs. Betty Reed, my high school business teacher, provided the support and encouragement I needed during my junior and senior years. She nurtured the qualities that would sustain me throughout my life's journey. This memorable lady influenced the 2002 graduating class' decision to ask me to deliver the commencement speech that inspired this book. I was deeply saddened by her passing in 2009.

Debby Yoder, one of my oldest and dearest friends: You've always been an inspiration, and it was your persistent encouragement that finally kicked me in the behind and motivated me to get this book done! Your idea for the title was brilliant, my friend!

Marcia Miller, another longtime Texas friend: Your support and advice on the commencement speech was deeply appreciated. Listening to me practice so many times entitles you to a medal!

Don Walsh, my dear friend and former KPMG colleague, gave me the final push I needed to quit my job and travel. My sabbatical was a significant milestone in my life, and I owe much of that to him. His advice and counsel have been sorely missed.

To the James Bowie graduating class of 2002 who graciously endured listening to the speech that inspired this book: Thank you and accept my belated apologies for going past my allotted time on your important evening.

Debby Yoder and Tony Martin: Thank you for traveling all the way to Colorado to assist me with one of the many revisions.

My friends Pat McLellan, Debbie Williams Jones, Linda Gaulden: I am indebted to you all for your listening ears and friendship.

Lisa Albro and Rebecca Hill: Many thanks for your writing guidance and counsel.

Barb Tobias, my Thrift Diva friend: Your counsel on this 2nd Edition was exceptional, your expertise tremendous and your friendship … priceless.

Ronnie Moore: Working with you on the layout was educational, inspirational and downright fun!

Nick Zelinger: Your vision and patience in creating a stunning cover were amazing.

Tim Hewitt: Thank you and the Friesens' team for your printing expertise.

Sharon Wright: My fellow Denver, Dallas Cowboys fan: Your professional direction was the winning touchdown; your friendship was the extra point.

John Maling and Judith Briles: Your editing, book shepherding and advice made the first edition of this book possible.

To all my cherished friends and family members: Although I've not specifically named you here, I hold you dear to my heart. You have all played a significant role in shaping the person I am today, and I love you for that precious gift.

To those who painstakingly read, reread and advised me on this manuscript: I am indebted to you for your support and encouragement.

Lastly, thank you Readers for the privilege of sharing my journey with you.

Contents

1. Setting Sail—Pirates on My Mind   1

2. Success—It's Not a Birthright   15

3. Determination and Perseverance—
   How Tough are You?   35

4. Attitude, Not Altitude   63

5. Success Is a Journey, Not a Destination—
   Enjoy the Ride   71

6. Give Yourself Permission to Fail—You
   Haven't Stopped Breathing Yet   79

7. Find Your Passion; Live Your Dream—
   The Wal-Mart Effect   89

8. Commitment to Live a Balanced Life—
   Carpe Diem (Seize the Day)   99

9. So Many Life Lessons   125

10. From Simms to Zanzibar—
    What the Heck Does That Mean?   133

11. Bringing It Home   143

12. Lynn's Notes (Way More Interesting
    than CliffsNotes™)   147

Foreword by the Author

In the two years since publishing the first edition of my book, *From Simms to Zanzibar*, I've received numerous letters, emails and comments that have been touching and heartwarming. The origin of the book was a high school commencement speech I was asked to give at my alma mater, a small high school in Northeast Texas. Given the topic, I mistakenly thought my audience would be graduating students from high schools and colleges. Much to my gratification and surprise, people of all ages have connected with my message and journey. This second edition has been updated and revised with the goal of reaching more readers who may gain valuable insights into their own lives and the paths they choose to travel.

When I lost my job in early 2009, I took the opportunity to write this book. The first printing was delivered on a Friday afternoon in May 2010; the following Monday, I received two job offers after 17 long months of unemployment. This propitious timing reinforced my sentiment that I had been gifted with an assignment to share my journey and touch lives.

Lynn McLeod, November 2012

You don't want to spend all your life climbing a ladder only to reach the top and realize that it was leaning against the wrong building.

—Anonymous

1

Setting Sail—
Pirates on My Mind

James Bowie High School Emblem
Home of the Pirates

I t was May 9, 2001, and I was minutes away from enjoying a three-day sailing trip through the Whitsunday Islands off the coast of Australia. Checking my email from a local Internet station, I was stunned—and extremely honored—to find an invitation to deliver the commencement speech at my alma mater. The ceremony, scheduled for the following week in Simms, Texas, was literally on the other side of the world.

Since my graduation from James Bowie High School in 1971, I had periodically returned to Simms to speak to Mrs. Reed's business classes. She encouraged me to share my stories with the hope my path would inspire the students, and encourage them to continue their educations.

She always said that I was her "Cinderella Story." But, those sporadic visits came to a screeching halt when Cinderella packed her glass slippers and left Texas in 1997.

A Commencement Speech a Week and an Ocean Away!

I began calculating the logistics of getting back to Texas in short order, wanting very much to be standing in front of that podium in seven days. I just couldn't figure out how I could make it from Airlie Beach, in the middle of Australia's eastern coast, to Sydney, to Los Angeles, to Dallas, to Simms, Texas ... in one week. It may be a small world but unless Bill Gates or Richard Branson was willing to whisk me away from the wilds of Australia on a private jet, it looked like I was stuck.

As I contemplated my situation, I realized that distance and short notice were the least of my concerns. What about that commencement speech?

Give a speech? Me?! What could I say to a class of graduating seniors? Furthermore, my glass slippers were getting fairly crusty and starting to crack. After all, I had left a perfectly good job with Siemens Medical eight months earlier to frolic around the world. All of my worldly possessions resided in a storage unit in Dallas; I had no apartment, no condo and no house. To put it succinctly, I was unemployed and homeless.

Thus far, my self-imposed sabbatical had been one continuous adventure; mountain climbing, backpacking, camping, sailing, snorkeling, hiking, biking, diving and river rafting. I had logged tens of thousands of miles on various modes of transportation. I was a modern-day gypsy sporting a backpack.

Mrs. Reed had known me as a girl longing for stability. Today, my friends laugh over that picture. I am financially comfortable and have a thirst for adventure that cannot be quenched. Traveling the world has been the fulfillment of a lifelong dream. So, when I received that email, I was not ready to return to the real world … not yet.

No Way!

I declined the invitation with heartfelt regret and offered to speak the following year for the James Bowie High commencement.

My scheduled sailboat tour departed with me resolutely stowed away. As I sailed around the Whitsunday Islands soaking up the sun and feeling the serenity of the crystal clear waters of the Pacific, pirates invaded my thoughts—the James Bowie High School Pirates that is. I couldn't help thinking about that speech … what I could say to graduating seniors.

With the days growing shorter and winter fast approaching, I realized that all my winter clothes were stored in a portable closet in the States. I decided to end my trip abroad in June of 2001 and make the long journey home.

I had no job waiting, no home to return to, no responsibilities. Therefore, I spent a couple of months visiting friends and traveling from Los Angeles to New York to Cape Cod to Texas.

The only place I could call home was the storage facility in Dallas. Well, at least that's where all my belongings resided. Clearly, gypsy or not, a windowless storage unit was not going to provide me with the comforts of home.

My dear friends from Atlanta, Tim and Jane Kelly, took note of my situation and rescued me with an offer to crash in their vacation home nestled in the Blue Ridge Mountains outside of Asheville, North Carolina. I retrieved a few things from my storage unit and headed north.

The Kelly mountain retreat was a godsend; a comfortable, three-level house tucked into the side of a wooded hill, it boasted a wonderful wrap-around deck that was perfect for contemplating my next move.

My Checkered Career

I had plenty of time to think about my life and my career path. I am a Certified Public Accountant with an MBA in accounting and taxation. After graduation from college, I went to work for one of the Big Eight firms, KPMG, and stayed for six years. Back then, they were the "Big Eight"; now they are fondly referred to as "The Final Four."

The next seven and a half years were spent in the offices of Trammell Crow Company—a prominent real estate firm in Dallas. Although I decided to take my career in a different direction in 1993, I still keep my CPA license current. Anyone who has ever sat for the CPA exam will understand why I continue to pay my professional dues. I may never practice again, but I worked hard, and I'm proud of that license that hangs on my wall.

From Trammell Crow I decided to go into sales. Now, that is not a natural career transition for tax professionals, but after almost fifteen years of living around IRS tax deadlines, I was ready for a new adventure. I found a position with Siemens Medical Systems in Dallas, Texas, doing healthcare financial sales—equipment leasing.

It was late August 2001 and I was still contemplating my future as I basked in the reverie of the North Carolina wilds. I'd been out of high school for 30 years and for the first time in my life, I had no strong inclination to live in any particular place. Although I considered Dallas my hometown, I wasn't ready to return.

It was time to go back to work, but where? Prior to my sabbatical, my jobs had taken me to New York, Colorado, Germany and New Jersey. The one place I knew I did NOT want to live was Los Angeles. My travels there left me with the impression of a sprawling metropolis, murky with smog and insane freeways.

California boasted the third-highest income tax rate in the nation, and real estate prices were out of control. Other than that, I had no problem with it ... really.

Los Angeles—Here I Come

I began searching for jobs in New York City, thinking that living in Manhattan might prove to be another adventure. Although I knew that real estate prices and taxes in the Big Apple weren't exactly IN control, I thought I'd give it another try. I had lived there in the early '80s when I worked for KPMG and knew how to navigate the city. Taking on Manhattan is like living in no other city—it demands patience and tolerance. There is even a proper way to order a beer in Yankee Stadium.

Still tucked away in the North Carolina woods, I spent my days job searching—on the Internet and telephone. Then on September 11, 2001, terrorists attacked the World Trade Center and the Pentagon, changing the world as we knew it. It also changed the way I viewed my future. The day before the tragedy, I had set up an interview with a company whose offices faced the World Trade Center.

I faced some serious questions: Did I want to work at Ground Zero? Was I willing to sacrifice my lifestyle for a job?

The truth was I needed to work. Traveling for a year on my reserves had taken a financial toll.

So, where did that leave me? Did I want to pursue a life in Asheville? Hmm, I had done stranger things—most notably, quitting a good job to travel the world.

The one thing I knew was I needed to work. However, finding employment post 9/11 took longer than I had anticipated. Even with my CPA and financial sales background, it was tougher than I expected.

I proactively pursued a position with GE Capital, which had offices throughout the nation. When I finally received "the call" offering me a position, I abandoned all thoughts of staying in the peaceful Blue Ridge Mountains. I was so excited to receive the offer that I never thought to ask where I would be located. The two dreadful words, "Los Angeles," hissed across the phone like a striking snake.

The hiring manager, hearing my hesitation, quickly offered me San Francisco. I agonized over the southern versus the northern location for a few days, checking the cost of living in both. Southern California was marginally more affordable, and the swing vote was having three sisters who lived there. When I called to say I was relocating to a place I would NEVER live, their laughter and joy were clear.

In January 2002, I moved to Newport Beach and

found a place that was so close to the office that I didn't have to commute on the parking lots they grudgingly call freeways.

The (E-Mail) Postman Always Rings Twice

In the midst of the upheaval, I gave little thought to my offer to speak at the James Bowie High School commencement. It was now March 2002, and my email delivered another invitation to speak in May. This time I had more lead time and was no longer lounging on a sailboat in the Pacific Ocean. But ... I was still confronted with the weighty task of what I would say to a group of graduates post 9/11.

The Challenge ... A Graduation Speech

What was important to high school seniors? Where did they see their life taking them? Should I use humor?

I felt my former teachers expected me to articulate something profound ... Mulling over those questions really made me think about my life. I also knew I needed to be interesting enough to hold the attention of a group of seniors eager to get to their graduation parties.

So I began my research. I scoured the bookstores and online sites for anything related to commencement speeches. I was curious to find out what commencement speakers talked about since I remembered little of MY high school commencement speaker.

My research uncovered very little on speakers who gave commencement addresses. Most speeches of note were from college or university functions. Frustrated, I decided to go to the source. Emailing the president of the James Bowie 2002 graduating class, I asked Jessica Patterson what she thought her classmates would want to hear. Here's what she wrote back to me:

> *The nicest thing is that you are from our school and you have made a success of yourself. Sometimes it is hard to realize there is more out there than Simms, Texas. Anything you have to say will be fine.*

Jessica and her classmates wanted to hear from someone who had made a success of themselves. I thought about my life ... thus far. How did I view success? What did that mean to me? And, who should I compare myself to? Bill Gates? Oprah Winfrey? Ok, so that was clearly unreasonable, but how does one gauge if someone is successful? Their wealth? The state of their business? Their accomplishments? Happiness?

Settling on My Subject

Over time, I realized that the subject of my speech was simply ... success. And, I actually had some ideas about achievement along with some tasty ingredients that are necessary to realize it.

So, now I had to face the age-old fear of speaking. Hmm, another hurdle. In a Time Magazine article (July 29, 2004) entitled "The Price of Pressure," author Sora Song shares a joke by Jerry Seinfeld talking about a survey saying that people are more afraid of public speaking than death! Seinfeld joked, "In other words, at a funeral, the average person would rather be in the casket than giving the eulogy."

Graduation Day

The desire to be in a casket never entered my mind, but my stomach was turning Olympic-sized somersaults sitting on the James Bowie High School stage waiting to speak to the graduating class of 2002.

After a nice introduction, I approached the lectern and looked out over a crowded gymnasium of expectant faces. A quiet calm came over me, and I began to speak … from my heart.

I was overwhelmed by the reaction to that speech. It was only afterwards, after people kept asking for copies of my speech, that the idea of writing a book began to take root. I realized then that we all have a story to tell. If I didn't write, no one would read. I had something to say, and I realized that I touched lives that night. I hope that this book will touch more. The speech is here (in shaded boxes) with a few additions to encompass "the rest of the story."

Why the Delay?

That was 2002; it is now 2010. You may be wondering what took me so long to write this book … Life! At the time of my speech, I was living in Newport Beach, then relocated twice for my job—first to Seattle, Washington, in 2004, and then, in 2005, to Golden, Colorado.

Ending up in Colorado was pure bliss. I spent a great deal of time skiing and playing in the Rocky Mountains over the years, and now living there felt like coming home. Of course, I will never relinquish my Texas passport—born a Texan, always a Texan.

Awards

Although my visits to Mrs. Reed's business class had come to an end, my desire to encourage young people to continue their education had not diminished. While sitting on that commencement stage in 2002, I decided to establish the Lynn Garrett Scholarship. My brother James joined me in 2008, and it is now the

Garrett Scholarship. We go each year to the graduation ceremony to present this scholarship to two deserving seniors. It reflects our deep conviction that education is a critical ingredient in living a fulfilling life. Education opens the portals to opportunity and choice.

In 2008, James and I went to the James Bowie graduation ceremony for another reason. We were honored with the James Bowie Distinguished Alumni Award. We've each received awards in our life, but none has meant more than that honor.

May 2010

*James and me
at the graduation.*

2

Success—
It's Not a Birthright

To laugh often and much; to win the respect
of intelligent people and the affection of children;
to earn the appreciation of honest critics and
endure the betrayal of false friends; to appreciate
beauty; to find the best in others; to leave
the world a little better, whether by a healthy
child, a garden patch or a redeemed social
condition; to know even one life has
breathed easier because you have lived.
This is the meaning of success.

—Ralph Waldo Emerson
American essayist, philosopher and poet (1803–1882)

Friends, family, parents, teachers and most importantly, the James Bowie graduating class of 2002!

The last James Bowie commencement I attended was my own ... on May 31,1971. I am deeply honored to be here and very pleased to be experiencing a significant improvement—this fabulous air-conditioned building.

My graduation ceremony was relegated to the football field topped with a stage made up of two flatbed truck trailers backed end-to-end. That was the only place we had for the ceremony because our gymnasium had burned down at the beginning of our senior year.

Looking Back

One cold, bleak November evening during my senior year, Mrs. Lavada Griggs, our normally stoic-faced, girls' basketball coach, stood with tears streaming down her face watching flames engulf our old gymnasium. The building was constructed from large, multicolored stones native to the area in the charming and distinctive style of a 1930s Works Progress Administration project. It had been the center of our athletic events, graduation ceremonies and various school activities. We knew, without the gym, we were up a creek with flimsy paddles.

Although a new facility was built the following year, it failed to recapture the grandeur of our old ally, and the image of our school was forever altered.

The gutted gym. By the light of day,
it was clear there was nothing to be
salvaged from the smoldering embers.

For those of us who played basketball, the ruin of this activity center was particularly devastating. For the remainder of the season, our team forfeited lunch and half of fourth and fifth periods to ride ten miles to

New Boston for practice. After our workouts, we would devour our stale lunches as we bumped back to James Bowie in an old yellow school bus.

We were a novelty to the students of New Boston High School since they did not sponsor a girls' basketball team. The pounding of the basketballs and the whistles from our coach drew scores of gawkers into the gym. Imagine how embarrassed we were when we missed a simple layup, or worse, when we got the order from Mrs. Griggs to run laps for committing some basketball faux pas.

So disruptive were we that, eventually, the New Boston principal declared the gym off limits to his entire student body during our practice sessions.

In spite of the loss of our gymnasium, our team had a banner year and ended up winning the Bi-District Championship.

As graduation approached, the gym was still a heap of rubble. Wanting to preserve the tradition of holding our commencement exercises on school grounds, the senior class, along with our faculty sponsors, discussed our options. Unfortunately, there was no building on campus large enough to accommodate a graduation ceremony. Eventually, two flatbed truck trailers were found, moved onto the football field, backed end-to-end and served as a workable, if not grand, stage.

Lack of Gym Didn't Stop Piratettes

James Bowie Girls Went Long Way on Borrowed Facilities

SIMMS, Tex. — The James Bowie Piratettes did pretty well this season — considering the girls didn't have a home gymnasium in which to practice.

Coach Lavada Grigg's Piratettes won 20 of 24 games this season, commuting to New Boston each day for practice after fire destroyed the James Bowie gymnasium November 17 of last year.

Paced by the scoring of senior forward Lynn Garrett and sophomore forward Rita Duren, the Piratettes captured the District 17-A North Zone championship. During the season they entered three tournaments, winning two. The Piratettes defeated Avinger to win the Redwater tournament and took the UnionHill tournament by beating Harleton in the finals.

The James Bowie girls annexed the 17-A title by whipping Harleton, 39-35, in the zone playoffs and Rita Duren and Janice Davis scored 16 and 15, respectively.

Next the Piratettes took on Hawkins in bi-districts action at Daingerfield. James Bowie emerged victorious, 61-51, as Lynn Garrett scored 26 points and Janice Davis 24.

Cushing finally stopped the streaking Piratettes in the regional playoffs last week in Brenham. Cushing won, 50-36, despite 16 points by Duren and 14 by Garrett.

Four seniors played their final game for the Piratettes against Cushing. They include forwards Davis, Garrett, and Kathy Hanna, and guard Cathy Granberry. The team also loses Mrs. Griggs who plans to retire after this school year.

The Piratettes have the material returning next year to have another fine team, but people in Simms will probably never forget the 1970-71 Piratettes who overcame the obstacle of not having a gym to have one of the finest seasons in several years.

BI-DISTRICT CHAMPS — The James Bowie Piratettes won the bi-district crown with a 61-51 victory over Hawkins before losing to Cushing in the regional playoffs. Members of the team include, top row left to right, Janice Davis, Cathy Granberry, Coach Lavada Grigg, Barcie Bryan, and Bonnie Granberry. Middle row, Rita Duren, Sandra Meadows, Kay May, Kathy Hanna, and Linda Duren. Bottom row, Lynn Garrett, Diana Whitecotton, and Anna Granberry.

#13—That's me!
"Paced by the scoring of senior forward Lynn Garrett and sophomore forward Rita Duren…"
Reprinted by permission of the Texarkana Gazette, Texarkana, Texas.

On May 31, 1971, our parents, teachers, friends and families gathered on the bleachers to watch us graduate. At that time of the year, only East Texans can imagine how hot and uncomfortable it was. Our long, dark-blue graduation gowns soaked up the sun, and we felt like we were sitting in a sauna. It was obvious that our audience wasn't faring much better as they sat red-faced, fanning themselves with their programs.

As I walked to the podium to deliver the Salutatory speech, I was certain everyone was hoping it would be very short. It was!

Giving the Salutatory speech, May 31, 1971. Notice the lovely wheels of the truck trailer.

Some things never change. Thirty-one years ago I'll bet most were thinking, "Jeez, I hope this speaker doesn't talk all night!"

One of Winston Churchill's most famous speeches was a mere nine words; "Never give in, never give in, never, never, never. Then he sat down. I briefly considered emulating him, but since I traveled 1,582.95 miles to get here, I hope you don't mind if I say a few more words than that tonight. In case you are wondering, that is MapQuest's distance from my home in Newport Beach to Simms, Texas.

I would like to show you something I found during my recent move to California: My James Bowie basketball letter jacket. Not bad for 31 years old, huh? The jacket that is....

As I continued with my talk, I pulled my jacket out of a bag resting at my side and put it on for the first time in 30 years. At 5'2" and only a few pounds heavier, I slid into it with ease. Each varsity player had been awarded a jacket. Mine had a special patch. I was proud to be selected as an "All-District" basketball player in my senior year. At 5'2" not many people would have believed that I could play basketball well enough to earn that patch.

My basketball jacket—it fits!
I've always thought that 13 was
my lucky number.

In 1971 we were leaving high school to begin our future in a country torn apart by war ... Vietnam. Today, you are entering a world united in a war against terrorism—a much scarier proposition in many ways.

The Vietnam War remains one of the most controversial conflicts in American history. Unlike previous wars, patriotism was not a motivating factor for enlistment. Few wanted to risk their lives in the jungles of a country most of us had never heard of, and few of us understood.

Participation in the military was mandatory during this war-torn time, and for this reason the government established a national lottery.

A No-Win Lottery

On July 1, 1970, my high school sweetheart, Doug Henry, and I watched nervously as the numbers were drawn, determining who would be called to serve in the Vietnam War.

Glued to that televised event, we realized that our fates would be determined by the random selection of the little blue capsules that churned ominously in a huge vat. Each container held a date of birth. If for example, you had a birth date of September 5th and that date was the first one drawn from the bin, you might as well start packing.

Doug's birth date, January 19, was the 188th number drawn—low enough to cause some concern since men assigned numbers reaching 195 were called to serve in the 1969 lottery.

Eventually, Doug did go through pre-induction exercises, but the highest number called from the 1970 group was 125. Some of our other friends were not so fortunate.

At the time, few of us truly understood the implications and consequences of this unpopular war. We certainly didn't have CNN showering us with horrendous images of the daily conflicts raging in that tiny country. The nightly news dedicated a few minutes each evening, but not to the extent that television does today. Because of that, it was much easier to put the war in the back of our minds and continue with our daily lives.

In 2001, I traveled to Vietnam during my sabbatical. Only then did I truly appreciate that war's impact on our country and the physical impact it waged on Vietnam and her people.

I also felt a profound sense of shame and sadness for how little we regarded the efforts and lives of our returning Vietnam veterans. Books rarely make me cry, but Jan Scruggs' book *To Heal a Nation* that tells the story of the building of the Vietnam Veterans Memorial in our nation's capital, left me in tears. Thankfully, those fighting for us in Iraq and Afghanistan have been received with honorable homecomings.

Other things have changed since 1971.
Back then we listened to Led Zeppelin and
the Rolling Stones; today we rock to Jay Z,
LL Cool J ... and the Rolling Stones.

Back in 1971, no one could have imagined that
Mick Jagger would still be rockin' and rollin' in his
late '60s! That brings to mind Britney Spears at 60 ...
halter top and fishnet stockings ... yikes! But, hey,
look at Tina Turner—most men would agree that she's
still HOT at 70-plus. And ladies, let's not forget
George Clooney—now in his 50s, he's still VERY easy
on the eyes.

We watched channels three, six and twelve,
assuming the antenna was positioned just right.

You have—what is it now—500 or more
channels for viewing opts? Our mail took a week;
now, "You've Got Mail" flies
across the world in milliseconds.

I laughed at myself later for having said this; it sounded like the adults I vowed, as a child, never to be like; they had all walked ten miles to school in the snow … barefooted, carrying their books uphill … yadda, yadda, yadda.

In 1971 we didn't have cable TV, Internet, email, computers, I-pods, PlayStations or cell phones. As a matter of fact, FM radio stations weren't common. We could, however, tune into WLS, an AM radio station out of Chicago, after dark when they cranked up their transmission power. My grandfather, with whom I lived during high school, didn't own a TV or a telephone.

The term "couch potato" was nonexistent as we actually had to get up to change TV channels.

Neighbors who did have telephones had to share a "party-line." If you wanted to catch up on community gossip, all you had to do was listen in.

Call waiting meant we were waiting our turn to make a call on the party-line. And, caller ID wasn't even a distant thought in 1971. When we answered a phone, it was like pulling numbers out of a Bingo bin—you just never knew who you were going to get.

Imagine having no Internet. I used to spend hours at the library looking up things in reference books.

No computers or email? Letters were sent via the U.S. Postal Service—with a real eight-cent stamp.

No I-pods? We had 8-track tapes and vinyl records (45 RPMs) with huge speakers that made the music sound like it had a bad cold.

No PlayStations or video games? Imagine having to find alternative ways to occupy ourselves! I read a lot of books, rode horses and bicycles with friends, went to an occasional movie in town and attended the activities at the Old Salem Church.

Microwaves were still electromagnetic waves, not something to cook with.

Icemakers were the metal ice trays that froze water in the freezer compartments of a refrigerator.

There were no non-smoking sections. Anything went as teachers smoked in teachers' lounges, and movie-goers puffed away while crunching popcorn.

There were no "Xerox" machines—only mimeograph machines that left ink on your hands and clothing.

But we did have S&H stamps—the original rewards program! Founded in 1896, Sperry and Hutchinson Company issued stamps for purchases made at supermarkets, gas stations and various retail stores. Once a book was full, it could be redeemed for products in the S&H catalogue.

We also had glass soda bottles! There were no poptop cans to break your fingernails or plastic bottles to scar our landscape.

Animals played a large role in our leisure time. We amused ourselves by agitating the bulls in the pasture, racing to clear the fence before they butted us, and we chased those odd-looking creatures called armadillos, knowing they could smell, but not see us.

While running after horses barefooted in the creek bottoms or swimming in muddy waterholes, we knew to strategically avoid water moccasins ... slimy reptiles indigenous to the area.

I finally did fall prey to one of those repulsive critters on a camping trip. A cotton-mouthed water moccasin slithered into my tent—no fancy zippers back then—and wasn't happy when I disrupted his comfortable sleeping place. He struck out and bit my arm, barely missing my face. I never saw my grandfather react so quickly and drive his old pick-up truck so recklessly as he sped me to the hospital! I don't know which was worse, my snake bite or the stress of Grandpa's speedy driving!

No cell phone? Imagine being out of touch with friends and family for more than a few hours! Now, if I leave the house without my cell phone, I feel like a cowgirl without her boots. One of the tragedies inherent in being out of communication was that I was out of town when Grandpa passed away. I didn't learn of his funeral until two days after his burial.

At the risk of sounding like a history book, here are a few other notable changes in pop culture over the past 40 years.

Internet dating changed the way we connect with people. If you lived in Texas, meeting and dating someone from New York City—or even France—was darned-near impossible. Now all you need is access to the Internet to shop for a dinner date, a hiking buddy or your soulmate.

"I'll have a cup of coffee please" is now met with, "Will that be a Vente or Grande," and often coupled with, "Would you like a double shot with caramel flavoring or just a macchiato?"

Then there is Reality TV ... say what??

As an aspiring CPA, I used adding machines; ubiquitous office equipment used to add and subtract. Today we use calculators ... or our smart-phones.

When I was asked to speak at this function, I struggled with what to say. In 1995 Bill Gates the Chairman of Microsoft, spoke at his high school commencement and spent an hour talking about the future of computer technology. Not only am I not qualified to talk on that subject, if I stand up here talking for an hour, I think you'll probably just shoot me. [Some clever senior called out, "Yes, we would!"] So by looking around, I figured that the best approach is to keep it simple.

Success is a relative term—it means different things to different people. For example:

Troy Aikman, former quarterback of the Dallas Cowboys said, "Success is not so much what we have, as it is what we are."

Colin Powell, while serving as Secretary of State, said, "Success is the result of preparation, hard work and learning from failure."

Oprah Winfrey said, "All the money in the world doesn't mean a thing if you don't have time to enjoy it."

Mary Kay Ash, founder of Mary Kay, Inc., one of the most successful cosmetic companies in the U.S., said "The real success of our personal and businesses lives can best be measured by the relationships we have with the people most dear to us—our family and friends. If we fail in this aspect of our lives, no matter how vast our worldly possessions or how high we climb, we will have achieved very little."

(*continued on next page*)

Ever heard of anyone wanting their tombstone to say, "He lived a good life ... but he wishes he could have worked another 1,000 hours!" I don't think so.

My personal favorite is by Booker T. Washington: "I have learned that success is to be measured not so much by the position one has reached in life as by the obstacles which he has overcome while trying to succeed."

Quoting everyone who has stated their opinions on success would fill another book. As I said in my speech, Booker T. Washington is my favorite. He lived from 1856 to 1915, faced tremendous obstacles and rose to become a prominent educator and leader of black Americans. Born into slavery, he was not allowed an education. But after President Lincoln issued the Emancipation Proclamation, he found himself free ... with nowhere to go. He held a backbreaking job in the salt mines of West Virginia until the age of 16. It was then that his craving for an education led him to the Hampton Institute in Virginia where he earned his teaching degree.

In 1881, he became the principal of the Tuskegee Institute in Alabama. His work helped make both himself and the school world-renown. As Martin Luther King, Jr. said years later ... he had a dream—that black people would be treated equally and would be allowed to improve their economic and social positions. His life was relatively short—59 years—yet his influence was profound.

I certainly would never place myself in the same class with Booker T. Washington, as my obstacles were "molehills" compared to his "mountains." While my economic position made getting an education more difficult, I at least had options. At the age of 16, I worked at the local Dairy Queen for seventy-five cents an hour, which was better than a job in the salt mines.

My success hasn't come easy, but I have to say, the longer the journey; the sweeter the success.

My definition of success, that I am going to share
with you, is based on a wide variety of life
experiences. However, if I leave you with
just ONE insight tonight—
then my 1,582.95 mile journey has been worth it.

3

Determination and Perseverance— How Tough Are You?

*I have often said that successful
people are just ordinary people
with extraordinary determination.*

—Mary Kay Ash
Founder of Mary Kay, Inc.
(1918–2001)

I wish I could tell you that I had my life all planned, and that I simply went out and systematically achieved my goals. But that's not exactly how it worked. When I was in high school I didn't waste time planning. Planning requires vision, and vision requires knowledge. The prolific author John Grisham once quipped, "Fifteen years ago, I had it all planned and thank goodness it didn't work out."

One day at the beginning of my senior year, our superintendent, Mr. John Meadows, called me into his office and told me I was the one senior awarded a $100 scholarship to attend East Texas Baptist College in Marshall, Texas.

Even though tuition was far less expensive years ago, $100 wasn't going to get me very far. I told him I appreciated the offer, but to please give it to someone who could use it. I needed full tuition money as well as capital for living expenses and a car for transportation.

The Scholarship

I lived with my grandfather during most of my high school years. He was retired and lived very simply, spending what little money he had on the basic necessities: food, shelter and electricity. We lived in a four-room house with no running water or indoor toilet. I rode a bus to school and depended on Grandpa, friends and relatives for transportation to school events, work, church and the like.

Most of the kids I went to school with were left to their own initiatives to advance their higher educations. There were few counselors to assist with scholarships, grants or financial assistance.

Today, through the dedicated efforts of educators like high school counselor, Dru Driver, many students at James Bowie High School are now seeking higher educations.

In 2008, there were more than 30 scholarships totaling $222,000 awarded to James Bowie graduates. In 2009, that number increased to 37 awards totaling an astounding $500,000. And, 2010 was even better with over $661,000 awarded!

Although I make it a point not to waste time playing "if only" ... if only those scholarship opportunities had been available when I attended school ... how much easier it would have been! By the same token, I think it was deprivation coupled with raw determination that made me passionate about pursuing and eventually achieving my college goals.

Multiple Roots

My birth-mother, Lee, abandoned me and my father when I was around nine months old, returning to her native California. Nineteen years later I met Lee for the first time. Although I had always been curious about my birth mother, our meeting proved to be a non-event.

I felt no connection to a woman I had just met. Sadly, my most vivid memory of that first meeting was that she was drunk when I arrived. Years later, one of my half-sisters told me that Lee was nervous about our meeting so she drank to "take the edge off." Even sadder is the fact that she drank every day—the day she met me was no special day.

Dad had remarried when I was four years old to the woman who raised, loved and nurtured me through my formative years. She was who I considered to be my real mom. Granted, Lee had given me birth, but it was my "Mother" who had given me a *life*.

Growing up, my father, BJ, my grandfather and extended family members told me bits and pieces of how I had come to live with them. Apparently, Lee enjoyed partying, drinking and a robust night-life—with little aspiration for much else. Having a new baby at the ripe age of 19 didn't fit into the lifestyle she enjoyed. She also wanted to return to California, and asked the Texarkana welfare office to take me.

When I met her, she defended having left me by insisting that my Dad was never around and she couldn't care for me. I didn't have the heart to ask the obvious question that had loomed in my mind all those years ... why didn't she just leave me with my father's family? In addition, when the welfare authorities took me, I was actually living with and being cared for by my great-grandmother.

When Dad and my grandfather learned that I had been taken by the authorities, they immediately devised a plan to rescue me.

Arriving at the welfare home, Grandpa worked to distract the nurse on duty while Dad walked out the door with me in tow. To keep the system from finding me, I was harbored in a distant relative's home in Ft. Smith, Arkansas. I lived with "Mamma Gail" and "Daddy Harvey" until Dad remarried.

When I was 20, I discovered that my name, during that time, was Alicia Nell. However, since everyone called me by my nickname, *Pumpkin*, I never knew I had another name ... another deep secret revealed.

When Dad married Dorothy, they took me back to Texas to live with them. I think I must have been a hyper-vigilant kid because, even with all the upheaval, I clearly remember a conversation I had with Dorothy soon after their wedding.

She sat me on her knee and spoke to me in a very adult voice. Lovingly, she explained, "I'm not your real mother; she lives very far away. But I love your Daddy, and I will love you and take care of you like you were my own little girl." That was the day she became my "Mother."

Although I was a normal little girl in most ways, I was also very observant. The first time "Mother" wanted to reprimand me for some childish transgression, I recall running around and around the car, under which my Dad was working, saying "Daddy, Daddy, she can't spank me, she's not my real mother." Needless to say, Dad and Mom both reminded me she *was* my mother.

Dad and "Mother" had two daughters of their own: Debbie and Patricia. Over the years, she never set me apart from her two biological daughters. She always introduced me as her oldest daughter, even after she and Dad divorced when I was 10.

When I visited my "Mother" in the hospital, where she eventually died of liver cancer in 1997, she proudly introduced me to the nurses as her oldest daughter. During one of those visits, I recounted the conversation we had when I was just 4 years old. Her eyes filled with tears as she expressed astonishment that I could have remembered something like that at such a young age. She passed away less than a week later. I'm eternally thankful that I had the chance to tell her how blessed I was to have had her as my Mother.

Mom and Dad divorced when I was 10, so between 10 and 14, I was shuffled between my grandfather, father, stepmother and step-siblings. Although my father was not always a constant figure in my life, I knew he loved me.

Lee, my birth mom, passed away in 2004. I sometimes wish that I had asked for her side of the story … or, maybe I really didn't want to know … or maybe I didn't believe she would share the truth.

Surprise—I Have a Brother

It turned out that my biological mother, Lee, was (surprise) pregnant when she left Texas. Eight years later the California welfare department notified my father that he had a son. Dad, a unique combination of parent and maverick, drove to California a few years later, bringing James, my new, eleven-year-old brother, back to Texas.

Today, Dad, at the ripe young age of 83, still enjoys a couple of 4,000-mile motorcycle trips with my brother James each year. Dad has always been a free spirit. Whenever he felt the urge, he would take off on his motorcycle while leaving me happily ensconced with Grandpa.

One time he moved us from Texas to California and back to Texas without even checking me out of school in California. So, I guess I inherited my responsibility gene from Grandpa. And, my free-spirit-travelitis gene definitely came from my Dad.

So there you have it: My life has been a roller-coaster of change. To give an example, by the end of the eighth grade, I had attended more than 20 schools from Texas to California. When Dad and Mom were married, we moved to California where I attended part of my first and second grades. Shortly after their divorce, I lived with relatives and attended part of fourth grade in Arkansas. An interesting side note to my school years is that the first school as well as the last school I attended was James Bowie School in Simms, Texas.

Stability at Last

In my freshman year I was in the throes of attending my second high school in one year. All of a sudden a hunger for some sense of stability descended on me. I decided to return, for the third time, to Simms, Texas to live with my grandfather and finish school at James Bowie High.

I had attended James Bowie for a portion of the first grade, and for the entire eighth grade. Understandably, I became known as the one "who always comes back." As a matter of fact, the eighth grade was the first time that I had attended one school for the entire year.

At the beginning of my senior year I was called into the superintendent's office. Mr. Meadows presented me with a senior ring … complete with my initials inscribed on the inside. I hadn't ordered a senior class ring. I even pretended that getting it was no big deal. The truth of the matter was I had no way of paying for such a luxury. I was dumbfounded.

"Who paid for this?" I asked.

"Your grandfather," he smiled in reply.

Sitting there overwhelmed, I fought the hot tears that threatened. I was afraid to show that fine man the depth of my feelings. Later on, when I was alone, I allowed the silent tears of appreciation to fall.

Although I never found out how my grandfather paid for it, I profusely thanked him, knowing that he had sacrificed something in order for me to have it.

My Valedictorian Medal for the eighth grade and my Salutatorian Medal for the twelfth grade … impressive medals for an unlikely kid like me!

In spite of all the changes, upheaval and moving around, I achieved Valedictorian rank in the eighth grade and Salutatorian status in the twelfth.

Dating? What's That?

I didn't date much in high school, primarily because both my father and grandfather were very strict. It was a bit embarrassing when they made the boys ask for permission to go out with me. Not many high-school-age boys have that kind of courage. I was also ashamed to admit, even to myself, that I was uncomfortable having people see where I lived.

In the summer preceding my junior year, I met Doug Henry, who not only asked my grandfather for permission to date me, but seemed unfazed by my lifestyle. His gracious attitude pressed me to reflect on the things I thought were important. Was it loving friends and loyal family members or indoor toilets and running water? Doug helped me see life in a different way. Although we broke up two years later, Doug remains one of my closest, lifelong friends.

Does Wal-Mart Carry Determination?

I've often wondered where determination comes from. Are we born with it? Does hardship breed it? Do mentors and family instill it? Did the love of my father and grandfather foster it? Can I buy it?

My childhood minister, A.M. Adams, once said that he believed my determination and resolve came from the fact that I was never told "You can't." I felt I had to prove something to myself, and to those who thought I had no chance. Whatever the reasons, I am eternally grateful for how it has played out.

Today I still believe that perseverance and determination are the keys to success. The November 10, 2009, edition of Time Magazine quoted a feisty 68-year-old Korean woman, Cha Sa-Soon, as saying, "You can achieve your goal if you persistently pursue it." After 950 tries, she finally passed Korea's written driver's license exam. Although I think I possess a high level of determination, I can honestly say that after about the 50th try, I might have just purchased a bicycle!

Motivation

The old house where I lived with my grandfather during my high school years still stands, dilapidated and sad—a stark reminder of all we didn't have. Even today, when I travel back to East Texas and pass by it, I feel profound sorrow for my grandfather. Somewhere deep inside I knew that I would someday drink water that came from a faucet rather than an old well and a battered dipper; that I would take a hot shower, or a bath in a clean white tub, rather than a sponge bath from a small basin; that I would walk on a soft pile carpet rather than cold worn linoleum. I wasn't sure how, when or where, but I knew.

My grandfather, on the other hand, was in the winter of his life—he passed away two years after I graduated from James Bowie and left home. I remember looking at his worn face and his cigarette-stained fingers, recalling my vanished dreams of buying him a house with an indoor toilet and running water.

My Grandfather's house in 2008. It doesn't look much different than it did in 1971.

My great aunt Alberta said to me many, many years later, "Your Grandfather and Father couldn't give you much, but they loved you." That said it all—they loved me and that has made all the difference in my life.

I had decided to go to Dallas after graduation—to do what? I wasn't sure yet. I just knew that my job at the Dairy Queen in New Boston, Texas, was not my future.

One of the girls I worked with at the Dairy Queen when I was still in high school was 21 years old. I remember wondering if she had aspirations beyond the Dairy Queen. Was she content or did she dream of something different?

One Saturday afternoon as I was dipping an ice-cream cone into the chocolate paraffin pot, I looked up and saw her cleaning the soft-drink machine, making a mess of her white Dairy Queen uniform. It was one of those defining moments. I wondered, "Is this my future? Is this all there is?"

Graduating to Dallas

I refused to accept the "yes" that hung in the back of my mind. I didn't know what the future had in store for me, but I did know with a deep certainty that my potential lay way beyond the parameters of that Dairy Queen.

My first decision was to begin my after-high-school life in Dallas. Since I had lived there on and off growing up, it wasn't a stretch for me to start there.

When I gave notice that I was leaving the DQ, Jerrod Elkins, the owner, said, "You'll be back."

I did go back. Approximately 10 years later, I walked up to the counter and ordered a soft drink. Jerrod waited on me. I could see that he was trying to place me. Giving me my change, his eyes searched my face. I said, "Jerrod, I'm back." A look of recognition slowly crept into his face. Shaking his head, he smiled and said, "But not to stay...."

"No," I smiled. "Not to stay."

I delayed going to Dallas for two weeks after graduation to give Jerrod an opportunity to replace me. I want you to know that at 75 cents an hour in 1971 I earned a whopping $50 to

(continued on next page)

start my new life. On June 16, 1971, I boarded a
Continental Trailways bus going to Dallas.
I had fifty bucks in my wallet, a smile on my face
and everything I owned in two of the ugliest
pea-green suitcases you can imagine. But, I didn't
have a clue as to what I was going to do.
Upon arriving, I experienced my first tough
lesson. A young man began chatting with me as
I was looking up my cousin's phone number. I
thought to myself, "What a friendly guy."

A few minutes later, that friendly guy was
running out of the bus station with my wallet …
all the money I had in the world. I just
became the poster child for the phrase
"not a penny to my name."

In those years they had pay toilets, and I didn't
have a dime to get in. Thankfully, a lady came out of
the stall and held the door open for me, saving me in
the nick of time.

> Then a kind gentleman at the information
> desk called my cousin, Dorothy Kyles, for me.
> She picked me up, helped me find a job and
> gave me a place to crash ... along with
> her husband and 4 children. Eventually
> I was able to afford an apartment I shared
> with two roommates.
>
>

I now realize how naïve I was at 17. Thinking back, I wonder what happened to that young thief in the bus station who felt he needed my money more than I did.

Every experience in life, good or bad, is an opportunity to learn a valuable lesson. Living with my cousin and her family in a three-bedroom house was one of those learning experiences. I realized that I should never fear asking for help if I needed it. Most successful people will admit that they have attained success due to the help and inspiration of others.

None of us got where we are solely by pulling ourselves up by our bootstraps. We got here because somebody bent down and helped us pick up our boots.

—Thurgood Marshall,
First black Justice of the U. S. Supreme Court

My First Job—Based on My High School Skills

I had envisioned becoming an executive secretary after graduation. My first job, a typist at Republic National Life Insurance Company in Dallas, seemed to fit my only marketable skill at the time. Mrs. Lasater, my business teacher until my junior year, had taken me under her wing and encouraged me to compete in typing and shorthand contests. Few remember shorthand today. It is a series of funny squiggly marks scribbled on paper and taken while someone dictates.

Thank you for reading my book.

Remember the old typewriters ... those monstrously heavy pieces of equipment that could have doubled as boat anchors?

I was thankful that I learned to type when my fingers were still supple and strong because the keys had to be struck hard enough to print. And, coordination was just as important. If the keys were hit too fast, big clumps of keys stuck together in a group. Those manual monsters were the epitome of agony and frustration.

An L. C. Smith
"Boat Anchor"

However, I became surprisingly proficient with the enthusiastic encouragement from Mrs. Lasater. Speed and accuracy were the answers to success. Although I could have easily lived without shorthand, I won several local and district contests.

After the bi-district wins, the state contests were held in Austin, Texas. I placed seventh out of eight people in my division in typing and eighth out of eight in shorthand. Not a particularly good showing, but I wasn't discouraged; just the experience of competing was worth the trip.

Yep, that's moi, holding my shorthand and
typing awards.
Awards … not so impressive.
Hair-do … priceless.

I've never underestimated the power of encouragement and positive reinforcement. The support I received from both of my business teachers, Betty Reed and Vivian Lasater, still warms my heart today.

Negative experiences are often more vivid … and destructive. My ninth-grade Home Economics teacher (from another high school) taught me how unfair and discouraging people can be.

During the first six-week semester of my freshman year, our class was instructed to sew a pair of pillowcases. I had been making my own clothes—skirts, blouses and such—for years, so a pair of pillowcases was a proverbial cinch. Not only were my pillowcases sewn perfectly, but they were completed five weeks earlier than the rest of the class.

I was stunned when I received a "B" and couldn't resist asking why, when others turned in pillowcases that had been unevenly sewn, ripped out and redone several times. Some had even received "A's."

I'll never forget her reply:

"It isn't fair to the other girls that you
already know how to sew."

Back then I was shy, so I suffered in angry silence. But, I determined never to settle for mediocrity again and learned to turn negative occurrences into positive experiences. I'm a firm believer in never letting others discourage you or keep you from realizing your dreams.

If Elvis Presley had listened to his music teacher at L. C. Humes High School in Memphis, he would never have become the King of Rock 'n Roll. He was told that he couldn't sing ... and was given a "C."

On My Own, at Last

Although I gratefully accepted my cousin's help when I arrived in Dallas, it didn't mean that I could continue to depend on her generosity. So, when the opportunity to move in with a couple of girls presented itself, I jumped at the chance.

I quickly realized that I was to experience another little life lesson. My roommates didn't understand the concept of privacy. They would park themselves on my bed to chat … cigarettes waving around in their hands. I didn't smoke … and, I didn't like it.

Later on I roomed with two male school chums whose idea of a clean kitchen was having a spot among the dirty dishes on the counter to set their beers. I guess one can't have everything … at least I had privacy within my own room.

Green—THE Color of the '70s

Remember those hideous pea-green suitcases? Although I stopped using them sometime in the late 1970s, there remained a soft place in my heart for those ugly appendages. Whenever I moved, I couldn't quite bring myself to dispose of them. They were noteworthy in that they carried everything I owned to start a new life. They were my "roots" in a manner of speaking.

As the millennium approached, I knew it was time to part with them. When I cleaned out my storage unit, I decided it was time to let go, and celebrated with a ceremony of sorts as I dropped them into the Dumpster. It was almost like parting with my childhood pet ... well not really.

*My green suitcases
... seconds before the
Dumpster devoured them.*

After I had been working for Republic National Life, my first job, for six months, I was able to buy my first car through the Credit Union. It was a bright chartreuse green sports car ... too small for my ugly pea-green suitcases.

It was the '70s and I was all decked out, finally mobile and on my way!

How I loved that car! There's something about "firsts" that have a profound effect on people—a bond of sorts: first boyfriend (fourth grade, Joe Richardson); first prom (junior year); first kiss (age 15, Danny Gonzales); first airplane ride (Texas International, 1971, Dallas to Houston).

That first car was a two-seated, Fiat 850, Spider convertible. I was finally free to move about the country, and move about I did. I luxuriated in the knowledge that I no longer had to depend on my roommates or coworkers to get me to and from work each day, or anywhere else for that matter.

My green car didn't end up in the Dumpster like my suitcases, but I realized I needed to let it go after a few adventurous years. Fitting more than two people in a two-seater was becoming a bit tiresome, not to mention dangerous. Ah, the days before seat-belt laws when we stacked three and four people in a two-seater. I realized that I needed a larger, more accommodating vehicle to fit into my changing lifestyle.

My chartreuse green,
1971 Fiat 850 Spider

"Movin' On Up": An Education and a Calling

At Republic National Life I started as a typist
then moved up to secretary. In 1971 that
meant taking coffee to my boss every morning.
It didn't take long for me to decide that I
needed to get a college education.

I began to think about subjects I enjoyed or had
an aptitude for, and thought back to the
accounting that Mrs. Reed taught me. And, it
wasn't long before I decided to go into accounting
and become a CPA. I thought, ... I can do this, and
realized that it took doing something that I didn't
like to spur me on to pursuing the things I did like.

So, I worked three jobs, saved my money and
started taking night classes at a junior college. A
year later I was able to quit my fulltime job, work
part time and go to school full time at North Texas
State University, now University of North Texas.

Looking back I must have been a great secretary
because my boss tried to dissuade me by saying
that I didn't need a college education. He tried
to sweeten the pie by saying that I'd probably
meet a nice young man and have a family.

(continued on next page)

> While he was saying that, I was thinking, "Yes, I can meet a nice young man, get married, have a family ... AND get a college education so someone can get MY coffee!" Am I missing anything here?
>
> Oddly enough, toward the end of my junior year, I realized that I didn't like accounting and I absolutely HATED auditing. Here I have spent all this money, time and energy focused on something I didn't really want to do. In my senior year I took my first tax course and breathed a sigh of relief ... I had found my calling.

It's difficult to explain the difference between auditing and tax ... kind of like trying to explain the difference between a good lawyer and a bad lawyer. A lawyer is a lawyer—a CPA is a CPA. The difference is in the details.

Actually, I was once told by an aptitude testing firm that I should never be an "accountant." Rather, I should be a tax advisor. They considered tax advising to be a creative discipline, whereas "accounting" was considered mechanical and repetitious. That may or may not be true. The truth is in the details.

Speaking of lawyers, many of my good friends are lawyers, so when I hear a good lawyer joke, I always have to tell it. Did you hear that lawyers are going to replace rats as laboratory research animals? That's because, one, they're plentiful; two, the lab assistants don't get attached to them; and lastly, there are some things that rats just won't do.

I continued my studies at University of North Texas and went on to receive a Masters Degree in Tax.

I started my new career with KPMG, one of the Big Four accounting firms, back when they were called the Big Eight. I believe they are now fondly referred to as the Final Four.

The moral of the story? I was determined not to spend the rest of my life carrying pea-green suitcases and driving a chartreuse car!

There is no way for me to know how different my life would be today had I taken a more proactive approach to my education and career choices early on. I didn't know about grants and scholarships. If only I had known … if only I had taken more steps … if only I had talked with more mentors. But, they are all pointless musings. Only Hollywood can recreate the past; it's totally up to each one of us to write the scripts for our futures.

Who's to say where I would be today–whether I would have chosen the same path– whether I would have been able to sustain a different track.

"Sliding Doors" is an intriguing movie that depicts in parallel format the path of a woman whose life is told in two different scenarios. One circumstance details a year after she misses a train; the other shows her catching the train (slipping through the closing doors).

Here's the SPOILER ALERT: In the end, although each path took her on a different journey, her ultimate destination was remarkably the same.

I like to believe that my life, despite my choices, is continuing to play out exactly as it should.

To borrow from Mr. Churchill:

> *Never give up; never give up,*
> *never, never, never!*

4

Attitude,
Not Altitude

I've learned from experience that
the greater part of our happiness or
misery depends on our dispositions and
not on our circumstances.

—Martha Washington
Wife of George Washington,
first President of the United States
(1731–1802)

I won't try to tell you that life is easy—
but it is really only as hard as you make it.
It's all about attitude. When you go jogging, do
you see the approaching hill as an obstacle, or an
opportunity to increase your aerobic capacity? Do
you passively accept not having money for college
as an excuse not to go, or do you subscribe to the
old adage, "Where there's a will, there's a way"?

One of the more difficult lessons we eventually learn is that life isn't always fair … as in not getting an "A" for sewing a perfect pillowcase. Life sometimes makes us do a sing-a-long without a song-book. Much of our life is simply a matter of how we handle adversity. Attitude determines your altitude!

Henry Ford, founder of Ford Motor Company, once said, "If you think you can, you can; and if you think you can't, you're right again." I find that people will get ahead much faster if they would simply abolish "can't" from their vocabularies.

Where There's a Will, There's a Way

When I graduated from high school, with no foreseeable path to college, I don't recall feeling defeated.

Somehow I knew I would find a way to get the education I sought. My attitude may have been a bit naïve given where I was coming from, but any other approach would have prevented me from even making the effort.

It is infinitely easier to keep an optimistic attitude when you surround yourself with positive people. Jack Canfield said in *The Success Principles*, "We become like the people we hang out with." Start to surround yourself with people you respect—people you want to be like—successful, affirming people.

I would never suggest abandoning longtime friends; just choose new friends with forethought and careful consideration.

If you find yourself in a negative position, try to diffuse it or make the choice to distance yourself from the situation. People who are negative can drain your energy and creativity. In the end, your attitude will be affected.

Getting an attitude adjustment may be overused, but everyone needs to do a reality check now and then. If I find myself becoming negative (yep, we all fall into that trap), stressed out and irritable, I take a time-out and ask myself a few questions:

- What about the situation can I control? What is beyond my control?

- How important, in the overall scheme of things, is the outcome?
- Is there another solution?
- Should I look at this from another perspective?

Then I go shopping. Well, maybe not, but I do find something I love to do that takes my mind away. I hike, I ski, I run—and well, OK, I shop sometimes.

The optimist sees opportunity in every danger;
the pessimist sees danger in every opportunity.
—Winston Churchill (1874-1965)
Historian, author and former
Prime Minister of Great Britain

Thomas Edison's ultimate invention of the light bulb is a study in positive thinking. He tried 2,000 different materials to make a filament. When nothing worked, his assistant complained, "All our work is in vain. We have learned nothing." Edison replied, "Oh, we have come a long way. We have learned a lot. We now know that there are 2,000 elements which we cannot use to make a good light bulb."

He looked beyond the obvious and continued to search until he found success.

Age is an Attitude

After a particularly long and tiring workout, my body fights the fact that life, or how we feel, is all attitude. Just because you are tired or growing older, don't let age be the single barrier to achieving goals and happiness.

Remember that Sam Walton was 44 years old when he opened his first Wal-Mart.

Ray Kroc was a mere 55 years old when he purchased a chain of hamburger stands from the McDonald brothers. The "golden arches" have since become an American icon that spans the globe.

Nola Ochs became the world's oldest college graduate in 2007 at the feisty age of 95. And, in 2010, she became the oldest recipient of a master's degree at 98.

In August 2012, Fauja Singh, at 101, became the oldest individual to complete a marathon. He finished the London Marathon in 7 hours and 49 minutes.

I am in awe of the 73-year old Japanese mountaineer Tamae Watanabe, who in May 2012, climbed to the summit of Mt. Everest, the highest mountain in the world. My 18,000 foot achievement on a nearby peak pales in comparison.

That's not to say that behavior, attire and circumstances should not be taken into consideration. Keep in mind that Mark Zuckerberg, founder of Facebook, purportedly made quite a stir on Wall Street when he showed up to meetings wearing a hoodie.

There is also something to say about age appropriate behavior. Not many people would enjoy seeing a 70 year old woman flaunting her midriff; or a 70 year old man braving a Speedo.

Age-appropriateness aside—attitude is everything. Age—it's an attitude.

A Lucky Attitude Adjustment

We all spend an enormous amount of time working. And, it's only natural that jobs, careers and managers affect our attitudes.

I remember one manager in particular that was driving me crazy. One Friday, after a particularly difficult and stressful week, I decided that I would resign on Monday. However, over the weekend I had a chance to think about the situation with a more rational mind. I decided that I would not let another person's actions force me into making an irrational decision. I decided to adjust my attitude and stick it out.

Within two months, my manager was asked to leave the company. I stayed on with that company for another three years, vesting in the profit-sharing plan.

Had I left in frustration, I would have lost money in the plan.

Christopher Reeves, in a wheelchair and paralyzed from the neck down, said, "You play the hand you're dealt. I think the game's worthwhile."

Shortly after a horseback-riding accident in 1995, Christopher was rushed to the hospital. He wished for death until the words of his wife gave him the will to live: "You are still you, and I love you."

I hope to never face a life challenge such as that, but if I do, I hope to handle it with similar grace and dignity.

You can complain because roses have thorns, or you can rejoice because thorns have roses.
—**Ziggy**
Comic strip character by Tom Wilson

5

Success Is a Journey, Not a Destination— Enjoy the Ride!

Focus on the journey, not the destination.
Joy is found not in finishing an activity
but in doing it.

—Greg Anderson
American author of "Cancer: 50 Essential
Things to Do" and a cancer survivor

Success is a continuous journey, not a destination. Former Dallas Cowboys quarterback, Troy Aikman, said that you can't measure success by what you have or how much money you make.

A person must look at the quality of their journey and the person they are. Do you treat people with compassion and dignity regardless of their station in life? What are your core beliefs? And, do you have the courage to stand up for what you believe, all the while remaining open-minded to others and their opinions?

Life isn't static—it happens on a continuum. It's a remarkable journey through time, comprised of countless experiences that ultimately define who we are. Does this mean that we should not set goals—not set benchmarks for success? Of course not! Businesses, at least successful ones, do not operate without a map (known as "goals" and "budgets"), so why should we?

Success Just Needs a GPS

Success is a journey without a destination ... a continual process of setting goals, achieving them and setting new goals. If you were to take a trip from New York to California, the trip would be a series of little changes … adjustments.

Life, like a trip, is continuously changing. We create small "destinations" by achieving goals—setting more goals—and reaching another destination. We determine the quality and direction of our journey by the decisions we make, the detours we take and the relationships we develop along the way.

The Success World is an infinite highway—many opportunities abound. This spot-on advertisement for Barclays Capital, an investment banking firm says it well:

> *Because success isn't a destination—it's a journey …*
> *on your road to success, we'll never ask:*
> *Are We There Yet?*

When I took that bus to Dallas two weeks after high school graduation without much more than a desire in my heart, my map was not a particularly clear one. My journey was filled with potholes, detours, downed bridges and even an occasional tornado. But each obstacle provided an opportunity and another life lesson.

Are you willing to accept and adapt to change? It's hard to imagine, but there was once a world without personal computers or the Internet.

I learned to type on an old manual typewriter ... then an electric one ... and finally on a computer keyboard. Learning is a lifelong process ... school may be out, but the classroom is everywhere and attendance is mandatory.

Gandhi once said, "Live as if you were to die tomorrow. Learn as if you were to live forever."

Peter Drucker, architect of modern-day management theories, said, "Today knowledge has power. It controls access to opportunity and advancement."

Those who think they know it all are very annoying to those of us who do.

—**Robert K. Mueller**
Twelfth director of the
Federal Bureau of Investigation

Education was my pathway to the quality of life I now enjoy. Classroom teaching was a good starting point, but I quickly recognized that every experience in life provided some element of learning.

I don't divide the world into the weak and the strong, or the successes and the failures ... I divide the world into learners and non-learners.
—Benjamin Barber
American political theorist

Travel and the Nation as My Classroom

One summer, on a break from college, a friend and I took a 6,000-mile road trip from Dallas, to Bangor, Maine, and back. That trip taught me more about American history than any class I ever took in school.

In every historical park we visited and every presidential home we toured, there was a film or other educational information that described the historical significance of the place.

One of the more interesting experiences we had was traveling from the Civil War historical sites in the South to those in the North. The perspectives of the Civil War represented at Andersonville, Georgia, one of the largest Confederate military prisons established during the Civil War, were notably different from those portrayed at Gettysburg, Pennsylvania, site of the largest battle fought during the war.

Andersonville only existed as a military prison for 14 months, but during that time, of the 45,000 Union soldiers confined there, 13,000 died from disease, poor sanitation, malnutrition or exposure. The battle of Gettysburg resulted in more than 51,000 soldiers killed, wounded, captured or missing. Those numbers are staggering. The South was fighting to preserve its way of life; the North to hold the Union together—divergent views within a two-day drive.

Driving farther north, we learned about the Revolutionary War. As we traveled down the East Coast, we visited Plymouth, where the Pilgrims ostensibly landed. I had to laugh at Bill Bryson who points out in his book, *Made in America*, that no reasonable mariner would dock a ship near a boulder on an open sea when there was a sheltered inlet nearby—not to mention that Plymouth Rock was most likely farther above water-line than it is today.

That trip was largely responsible for igniting my insatiable appetite for travel as a way to learn about places, people and events in history. Since then, I have traveled to 49 of the 50 United States. North

Dakota will round out my visits and explorations of the U.S.—not to mention more than 60 countries I've visited. There are more places to see than I have time and money for, but I continue to make valiant efforts.

"Imagination is more important than knowledge ..."

According to Albert Einstein, "Imagination is more important than knowledge, for knowledge is limited while imagination embraces the entire world."

I wish I'd said that. I think he was saying, "Think outside your box" ... never allow your life experiences, knowledge and education limit your imaginations.

Fred Smith had an idea. He created a worldwide revolution in mail and packaging services when he founded Federal Express in 1971. He had entered Yale University in 1962 and wrote a paper proposing a reliable overnight parcel delivery service. His professor's response was so-so. He told Smith, "The concept is interesting and well-formed, but in order to earn better than a 'C,' the idea must be feasible."

I often wonder what happened to that professor.

Focus on the journey; dodge the potholes.

—lynn

6

Give Yourself Permission to Fail— You Haven't Stopped Breathing Yet!

He's no failure. He's not dead yet.

—William Lloyd George
British peer and soldier

Remember the tagline from the movie "Love Story"? "Love means never having to say you're sorry." In much the same way, success means giving yourself permission to fail. Just like Winston Churchill repeated himself, I will take the liberty of repeating the same lesson; success means giving yourself permission to fail. Failures and adversities can be the foundation for success when you learn from them and build on your experiences.

There is plenty of literature on the subject of failure. Take a quick tour of Amazon.com and see how many results come up when you type in "failure." In January of 2010 alone, there were over 14,000 books which included "failure" in their titles. Here's a small sampling:

- *When Smart People Fail* by Carole Hyatt and Linda Gottlieb
- *Celebrating Failure: The Power of Taking Risks, Making Mistakes and Thinking Big"* by Ralph Heath
- *The Power of Failure: 27 Ways to Turn Life's Setbacks into Success* by Charles C. Manz

- *The Road to Success is Paved with Failure* by Joey Green
- *Great Failures of the Extremely Successful: Mistakes, Adversity, Failure and Other Stepping Stones to Success* by Steve Young
- *Woulda, Coulda, Shoulda: Overcoming Regrets, Mistakes and Missed Opportunities* by Arthur Freeman

Watch Out—Detours Ahead!

The highway of life is paved with disappointments, errors, missteps—and even those annoying potholes. As hard as we try to focus on the journey, we often let our frustrations and challenges delay our journey. The key is finding and embracing the detours.

These "bumps" are necessary for our growth and eventual success. When life is perfect, what is there to learn?

Failure is a part of success. There is no such thing as a bed of roses all your life. But failure will never stand in the way of success if you learn from it.

—Hank Aaron
Retired American baseball player

Deal With It—and Move On

Don't dwell on past failures. Rather, acknowledge them, embrace them, learn from them and move on. This is a true test of our character.

It is far better to dare mighty things and to win glorious triumphs, though oftentimes you are going to experience failures, than to rank with those poor people who neither enjoy much nor suffer much because they live in the shadow of life that knows no victory or defeat.

—Mary Kay Ash

Consider President Abraham Lincoln's path to the White House (from Steve Young's *Great Failures of the Extremely Successful*):

- Failed in business in 1831.
- Defeated for Legislature in 1832.
- Second business failure in 1833.
- Suffered nervous breakdown in 1836.
- Defeated for Speaker in 1838.
- Defeated for Elector in 1840.
- Defeated for Congress in 1843.
- Defeated for Congress in 1848.
- Defeated for Senate in 1855.

- Defeated for Vice President in 1856.
- Defeated for Senate in 1858.
- Elected President in 1860.

Whew ... I grew weary just reading about his failures—that many defeats would probably have prompted even me to throw in the towel. Abraham Lincoln exemplifies the power of courage and perseverance; enduring the swells and crashing of the waves of disappointment.

If at first you don't succeed, try, try again.
                                                    —Old adage
If at first you don't succeed, join the elite club
of those of us who make it up as we go along ...
until we do.
                                          —lynn's version

A few modern-day success stories are noteworthy. You might remember Lucille Ball from the "I Love Lucy Show." She moved to New York City at the age of 15, went to countless auditions, and was repeatedly told she had no talent. And, she was encouraged to ... go home. It is fortunate for all who loved her that she stuck to her dream. Lucille Ball was, by the way, the first woman to own a Hollywood studio.

Almost every book written by John Grisham has been made into a movie. However, more than a dozen agents and publishing houses originally rejected his first novel, *A Time to Kill*. That first attempt was self-published and was later sold to Fleming H. Revell, a publisher in Michigan, for $5,000. In 1996, it was made into a highly popular movie starring an assembly of A-list actors: Matthew McConaughey, Sandra Bullock, Samuel L. Jackson, Kevin Spacey, Donald Sutherland, Kiefer Sutherland and Ashley Judd.

Maybe not everyone has a failure-to-success story, but be assured that everyone has a story. What is yours? Where are you on your journey?

A few years ago, I was being considered for a promotion that I had worked hard for ... and felt I rightly deserved. A coworker was also being considered. As the decision time approached, it became apparent that the competition was becoming political.

During that uneasy time, I went to lunch with a colleague and he asked me if I REALLY wanted the position ... was it something I really

(continued on next page)

wanted to do, or did I want the advancement because it was "expected?"

I did some soul searching and when the decision was made to promote my coworker, I swallowed my pride, dusted off my ego and hung in there waiting for another door to open ... another opportunity.

Are you ready for another happy ending?

Within six months I was offered another position that I not only enjoyed more, but one that propelled me in a completely different direction ... sales! I loved it! My failure to achieve a cherished goal allowed me the opportunity to explore another.

A "Failure" Opened the Door to Success

The story I just related was one where I was being considered for a tax director position which I thought I wanted and deserved. When another coworker was chosen, I initially felt like a failure. I took it personally and focused on my limitations and my shortcomings.

However, after reflecting on the lunch conversation I had with my colleague, I was forced to be realistic about what I really wanted. The new position that popped up six months later was a special project that involved restructuring thousands of real estate partnerships holding millions of dollars of real estate assets. It was that opportune position that changed my career focus from tax to finance; the perfect segue to eventually transitioning into sales. My "failure" was an opportunity in disguise.

Downsized to "Rightsized"

In January 2009, my career took another detour. The financial turmoil of 2008 prompted my company to reduce its workforce ... and that meant me.

I became a "reduction" at a time when unemployment in the United States reached levels that had not been seen since the '50s. To add insult to injury, I was well past the 10th anniversary of my 40th birthday!

The Four Horsemen of Despair descended on me— anger, defeat, fear, failure. There's that nasty word again—failure. I did experience all those feelings as I stared at those Four Horsemen.

After a few long moments, I sent them galloping. I embraced the fact that I—and only I—could determine how I would react to my circumstances.

As it turned out, I received a generous severance package. I also had a bit of money saved, and a little time to spare, so my brother James and I took an adventurous vacation to Costa Rica and Nicaragua.

After that amazing trip, I settled into creating the next chapter of my life. I now had time to do things I couldn't do when I was immersed in the business world, most notably, finishing this book.

Failure is a detour, not a dead-end street.
—Zig Ziglar
American author, salesman
and motivational speaker

7

Find Your Passion;
Live Your Dream—
The Wal-Mart Effect

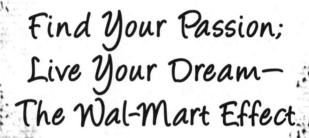

If people believe in themselves,
it's amazing what they can accomplish.

—Sam Walton
Founder of Wal-Mart, considered to be
the most successful retail company in the world

Some of you might have clear plans once you leave here tonight—a path that involves a chosen university, a job or perhaps a trade school. Others may be content to simply graduate ... while some may gamble on a Russian roulette game of life.

Regardless of your plans, great or small, I offer you this challenge; tomorrow, when you wake up, find something you are passionate about to pursue ... then, live it.

Don't be afraid to search for that vocation which sets you on fire ... throughout your life.

I started with a passion for taxation, only to discover, years later, that it was sales that inspired me. You will be infinitely happier doing something that YOU love versus doing what some other person thinks you SHOULD do ... trust me on that one.

Sam Walton may not be a name as recognizable as Angelina Jolie or Brad Pitt, but the retail chain he founded is so engrained in our culture that unless you've just finished a 40-year sleep, you've probably shopped or driven by a Wal-Mart store.

According to Charles Fishman in his book "The Wal-Mart Effect":

> *More than half of all Americans live within five miles of a Wal-Mart store, less than a 10-minute drive away. Ninety percent of Americans live within 15 miles of a Wal-Mart. On the nation's interstates, it is rare to go a quarter hour without seeing a Wal-Mart truck.*

Born in 1918, Sam Walton was already 44 years old when he opened the first Wal-Mart in 1962. Not only has it redefined the way we shop, but because of its undisputable dominance in the retail world, it has squeezed out an impressive list of competitors across the country.

Granted, many refuse to shop there, while others try to stop new stores from opening in support of smaller, local businesses.

On the other side of the fence, many find great pleasure in, not only shopping at the new SUPER

Wal-Marts, but simply enjoy browsing, much like the time I spend cruising a bookstore.

Regardless of one's position on the Wal-Mart phenomenon, there's no denying the mega-store touches our lives in some way.

A friend of mine, Kevin Francis, told me a story of a brief encounter he had with Sam Walton. Walton's words affected him so much that he still remembers his words to this day.

Kevin was a guest at the wedding of Sam Walton's granddaughter whom he knew from their college days. Unexpectedly, he found himself standing in the buffet line next to Walton. Wondering what to say to one of the wealthiest men in the world, he found that he was speechless. Much to his relief, Walton initiated the conversation by asking him what he wanted to do with his life. Since Kevin had just graduated from college, he replied honestly that he had no idea. However, recognizing that he had a once-in-a-lifetime opportunity to ask one of the world's most successful businessmen his secret to success, Kevin ventured, "Mr. Walton, what is your key to your obvious business success?"

Smiling shrewdly, Walton said that he was frequently asked that very question and that his secret is a lesson in simplicity:

Find something you love to do, set goals and
work like crazy to accomplish those goals.

You see, one man, Sam Walton had a dream: to build a corporation and culture that was unequaled in the modern business world.

Simply Success?

Find your passion; live your dream—straightforward in theory, but perhaps not so simple in execution. Although not everyone aspires to be a Sam Walton, most do want to know how to identify their passion.

When one Googles the word "passion," a variety of subtopics come up—from conferences to book titles. What is passion ... how does one find it? There is not a lot that defines a vocation or a "calling." The process actually takes effort and self-examination. There are a number of questions to ask when searching for that life purpose. Here is a small sampling:

- What do you enjoy doing?
- What gets you excited?
- What do you dream about?
- What are you good at?
- What kind of lifestyle do you want?
- What careers do you hold in high esteem?

- What kind of people do you want to associate with?
- What do you believe in; what are your core values?
- What do you have an aptitude for?

Sometimes it is a matter of knowing what you *don't* want, in order to arrive at what you *do* want in life. Many of us have taken aptitude tests. Aptitude is defined as a natural ability or talent. Earlier, I mentioned that an assessment company tested my preferences and penchants in order to determine what line of work best suited me. It was suggested that I become a tax professional rather than an accountant.

Now, keep in mind, this firm, over a three-day period, worked to identify and categorize my abilities. I knew that I *didn't* want to be an auditor. The tax field proved interesting for awhile, but it didn't take long for me to throw caution to the wind and change my career from tax work to sales.

Another lesson learned: it is necessary for each person to identify their own passions.

CNBC broadcast a town hall event at Columbia University, in New York City, on November 12, 2009, featuring Bill Gates, founder of Microsoft, and Warren Buffett, founder of Berkshire Hathaway. They are close friends and self-made billionaires. A student asked Mr. Buffett which industry he thought would produce another "Bill Gates" because that was the industry she wanted to find a job in. His reply was once again a lesson in simplicity:

> *Find what turns you on. Find what you have a passion for. If somebody said to me when I was getting out of Columbia, that Bill's business was going to be the one that would be exciting, I don't think I'd have done so well. But I knew what turned me on. I had a professor, Ben Graham; I offered to go to work for him for nothing. He said, "You're overpriced." Nonetheless, I went into the business. I will guarantee you will do well at whatever turns you on. There's no question about that. Don't let anybody else tell you what to do. You figure out what you are doing.*

In many cases, we follow vocations that we have been exposed to; for example, if your mother was an attorney you might look at the legal system. If your father was a schoolteacher you might pursue an education degree. I was good at bookkeeping in high school, so I thought accounting was a good idea, whereas the tax field turned out to be where my interests turned.

Then after awhile, my exposure to the sales profession changed my direction yet again.

Unlike years ago when people worked for a company for a lifetime, today it isn't unusual to have two, three or even four careers.

Sam Walton began his career with J. C. Penney, then owned and ran his own five-and-dime store, and eventually history was made with Wal-Mart.

Many famous actors and personalities held down various jobs before hitting it big. Harrison Ford was a carpenter, George Clooney a shoe salesman, Simon Cowell a mail clerk at EMI, Ellen DeGeneres a driver at a car wash and Faith Hill a receptionist at a music company.

The Road Less Traveled

My brother, James, traveled a different road. His passion for music and the arts dates back to his childhood. Although following artistic passions can be quite lucrative (think Brad Pitt), or not so lucrative (think "starving artist"), James traveled the artistic highway long before he decided to take the more conventional route. Against the advice of his CPA sister, James studied and earned a degree in accounting. Predictably, his lack of passion for accounting drove him back to his artistic pursuits.

Today, James headlines two shows in Branson, Missouri: a Tribute to John Denver and a second one featuring the music of several country music legends. He awakes each morning looking forward to going to "work." Although performing as a headliner did not happen overnight, and his road-warrior stories could fill another book, performing isn't work to James ... it's his passion.

Cross the roads you have to cross to get to the road you want to cross.

—James Garrett
Performing artist and brother of the author

Even in today's "instant gratification" society, "instant success" is highly improbable. I submit that patience, diligence and persistence are necessary attributes in the pursuit of dreams. Heck, I even looked for them in my local Wal-Mart ... and couldn't find them!

Every success in life, large or small, begins with an idea ... a dream. Passion drives it across the finish line.

—lynn

8

Commitment to Live a Balanced Life— Carpe Diem (Seize the Day)

> The tragedy of life is not that it ends so soon, but that we wait so long to begin it.
>
> —Anonymous

The last noteworthy ingredient of success is the commitment to living a balanced life. Unfortunately, too many people realize this element too late in life ... or never realize it at all.

You may not spend your free time reading the obituaries, but if you did, you aren't likely to find anything said about how many hours someone worked during their life. Rather, it is always about what a wonderful mother, father, daughter, friend or son they were.

There's more to life—like friends, family, fun, laughter and good health. With today's advances in medicine, statistically, your chances of living a longer and more productive life are greater than ever before ... so you have to prepare for a long life. But the cold hard fact is that TODAY is the only time we have ... for sure. Live like it. Cherish your family and friends TODAY, not tomorrow. Tell them you love them every time you see them!

Allow me to quickly review the elements of success I've discussion so far:

- Determination and Perseverance
- Attitude
- Success is a Journey, not a Destination
- Giving yourself permission to fail
- Finding your passion, living your dream

Living a balanced life is my favorite—albeit the most challenging element. In this era of fast-paced living, dedicating time to one's marriage, children, friends and extended family is difficult but so necessary. Add to that the need for fun, staying healthy and developing a spiritual life. It's no wonder we find ourselves overwhelmed. However, making these things a priority is critical to our well-being.

Family life, marriage, children and divorce are all subjects that have spawned an avalanche of books with experts dishing out advice ad-nausum.

With the divorce rate in the U.S. at almost 50 percent, it seems that people are too focused on their careers and getting ahead to give their relationships the attention they deserve. After all, committed relationships require attention, pruning, watering and grooming in order to bloom.

One can debate the many causes for the breakdown of relationships, but make no mistake; relationships and marriage require tremendous commitment and should be entered into only with clear and prudent forethought.

I have been married—and I have been divorced. However, I've only experienced having children vicariously, through my family and friends.

I have seen, firsthand, that these relationships are complicated. Although parents all love their children unconditionally, not one has ever said that raising children is easy.

Divorce—A Significant Segment of My Learning Curve

I am sure you are questioning how a divorcee, who has no children and no significant-other in her current life, would have anything of value to say about marriage and relationships.

Despite a person's status, they are constantly developing relationships in various stages and at different levels. And, there are many things I have learned over time; most importantly that there are three words that are critical to any relationship: Communication—Communication—Communication. Most things will take care of themselves if we just talk to one another!

My personal search has been interminable, but I've yet to find anyone who can read my mind.

I'm often asked why I'm divorced—as if I have a large "D" emblazoned on my forehead. My truthful response is: There is never just ONE reason—divorce entails a combination of factors. If I am hard-pressed to identify a single cause, I would say that the lack of communication heads the list.

Personally, divorce was an emotionally devastating experience ... one I would never wish on anyone. Although painful, in retrospect, it was another one of my many learning experiences.

When two people decide to get a divorce,
it isn't a sign that they "don't understand"
one another, but a sign that they have, at last,
begun to.

—Helen Rowland
Author of *A Guide to Men*

Friends and Friendships Can Save the Day

Friendships are important. After all, they are simply another form of relationships. Like marriage, friendships need to be cultivated, nurtured and valued.

Be a loyal friend. The older I get, the more
I realize the incredible value of true friendships.
You will meet many people in your life, but
your true friends are the ones who make an
indelible imprint on your heart.

Friends, although not biological, are like the "family"
... we choose. Eleanor Roosevelt wrote; "Many people
will walk in and out of your life, but only true friends
will leave footprints in your heart."

I have found this to be true. Over the course of my
life, I have crossed paths with a significant number of
people via school, career and travel that touched my
life in some way ... but those who touched my heart
are the ones I call friends.

As legendary actress, Marlene Dietrich so aptly
put it, "It's the ones you can call up at 4:00 a.m. that
really matter." True friends are one of life's most
precious gifts. We don't need to explain or apologize
for who we are because we've known each other
through good times, bad times and a few stupid times.
Those are the people I call at 4:00 in the morning.

I began a tradition 30 years ago that has proven to be a great way to stay in touch with family and friends. Keep in mind: This was pre-Facebook days. I made a point of sending holiday cards out every Christmas. About 15 years ago, I began sending photo cards. I choose one picture from one of my yearly treks and put it on my holiday card. Although this tradition has proven to be expensive and time-consuming, I get immense pleasure from friends telling me how much they look forward to receiving my card each year. But it's a bit like Hotel California; once you're on my list, there's no getting off of it….

A Friend May Have Saved My Life

A life-threatening experience in February 2006 gave the commencement speech I delivered new meaning:

> We are only guaranteed THIS moment …
> live it to the fullest.
>
>

My friend from Las Vegas, Pat McLellan, and I were backpacking with a hiking group on Aconcagua, the highest mountain in South America. I unexpectedly suffered a venous thrombosis, the formation of a blood clot in a vein, in the left cerebellum of my brain. The bleeding caused me to lose my equilibrium.

As the world spun, I began vomiting over and over. That retching process exacerbated, what I later learned, was a severe case of dehydration.

Although I had no idea what was wrong, I knew it was not altitude sickness; I had experienced that in the past and knew this was something more serious.

A helicopter was dispatched to transport me, along with a few altitude-sick hikers, off the mountain. An ambulance took me to a scary, sub-standard, health-care facility nearby where I uncomfortably awaited the arrival of my hiking group to take me to more hospitable facility. As sick as I was, the experience gave me a whole new appreciation for the United States, its healthcare system and its amenities ... broken as it may be!

As they loaded me into the helicopter, I couldn't help but think, "Cool ... a helicopter ride!!" Unfortunately I was too sick to enjoy anything beyond the take off.

Although I knew something was VERY wrong with me, I was unaware of just how serious my condition was. I simply remember being annoyed that my trip was being interrupted.

Upon my return to the U.S., I sought medical attention only when my symptoms persisted. My friend and colleague, Julius Fortuna, observed during a company sales meeting that I was not acting "right" and insisted I schedule an MRI. The MRI revealed the venous thrombosis.

My physician, Dr. William Orrison, determined the thrombosis was caused by severe dehydration and suggested I purchase a lottery ticket because I was, as he put it, "one lucky lady." I was fortunate to not only be alive, but had narrowly escaped spending the rest of my life in a wheelchair!

I vividly remember on my first hike following this trauma, standing on top of a Colorado mountain devouring the beauty, taking in the spectacle and giving thanks for the miracle of my recovery.

Remember how I talked about the importance of friends? It was in large part due to Pat's quick thinking that I am alive today. Not only is she a registered nurse, but a very determined gal (picture a beautiful pit bull with lipstick) who made sure the medics at base-camp put me on IVs, kept me warm and dispatched a helicopter. She searched for me in that dreadful healthcare facility even after she was told that I was not there. I will always take her call ... even at 4:00 a.m.

Reflecting on Mortality

A near-death experience forces you to think about your mortality ... and the joy of being alive. I was inspired to write a few songs about living and dying, only to discover that Tim McGraw and Nickelback beat me to it with their songs "Live Like You Were Dying" and "If Today Was Your Last Day."

That being said, if we truly lived each day like it was our last, we would never put off calling a friend, giving our loved ones a hug or putting money away for retirement. We wouldn't sit in front of a television or computer for hours, eat dessert last or acquire a home with a 30-year mortgage.

I think the message is this: Live a meaningful and happy life. Our time on earth is short, so make every day, every minute and every second count. Carpe Diem.

The way we treat everyone counts; our friends, business associates, aging parents and our children. Here is a tongue-in-cheek thought....

Be a good mentor and parent so that your children won't write a book about you!

Although that statement was meant to be a joke, consider the books written by children of famous people. These volumes often reveal sad incidents ... well-kept family secrets:

> *The Way I See It* by Patti Davis, daughter of
>   President Reagan
> *Mommie Dearest* by Christina Crawford,
>   daughter of actress Joan Crawford
> *A Paper Life* by Tatum O'Neal, daughter of
>   actor Ryan O'Neal

A Mentor in Time ...

Three or four years into my career, the partner in charge of the tax department at KPMG decided to "challenge" me, as his secretary put it. He began giving me assignments at the last minute which required working all weekend or, in some cases, all night.

One of my managers recognized my predicament and established a protocol whereby, unbeknownst to the partner-in-charge, he would assist me and review my assignments prior to completion. Now, that's what I call leadership! This wise man's actions not only bolstered my reputation in the eyes of the partner-in-charge, but also boosted my self-esteem and confidence. I've always remembered and appreciated his efforts on my behalf.

Mentoring goes beyond simple training—it also involves sharing experiences, facing challenges and offering support and encouragement.

Think about life as if you were sold on the idea of "paying it forward" ... every day. Become a mentor. Not only are you enriching someone's life, in the process, you are enriching your own.

In 2008, I became a mentor for a twelve-year-old girl through an organization called Denver Kids, Inc. This outstanding organization provides mentoring and counseling to underprivileged kids in the Denver Public Schools system.

Although Denver's graduation rate is alarmingly low—50 percent compared to the national average of 70 percent, the Denver Kids, Inc. program is able to graduate more than 90 percent of its students.

Its mission:

Denver Kids, Inc. helps students, grades K-12, who face the personal challenges of higher risk environments, to successfully complete high school, explore post-secondary options and become productive members of the community.

At a Denver Kids breakfast, the superintendent of the Denver Public Schools system, Tom Boasberg, delivered some startling statistics:

- Every six seconds, a student drops out of high school.
- The average cost of an individual dropping out of high school is approximately one million dollars over the life of that person in the form of lower income and government programs.

His concluding words continue to resonate with me, "Failure to graduate is condemnation to the second-tier economic level."

There are numerous ways to provide leadership, guidance and mentoring. It doesn't have to be through an organized group. Think about kids in your neighborhood whose parents both work and have little time to help with their children's homework. What about helping a coworker who is struggling with a difficult manager?

Also, don't confuse "mentoring" with "enabling." In the words of Abraham Lincoln, "You cannot help people permanently by doing for them what they could and should do for themselves."

Move That Body—And, Benefit Your Mind!

One last thought on living a balance life:
Strive to stay physically healthy! My participation
in sports at James Bowie started what has
become a lifetime commitment to fitness and
exercise. Remember my jacket? It still fits.

Sports were an important part of my life in high school. I played basketball, softball, volleyball and ran track. In college I discovered tennis, snow skiing, hiking and biking. Staying fit was not a problem during my peak activity years—then along came sitting at a desk, traveling, business dinners and not having time to go play. Ouch … where did those extra 10, well … ok, 15 pounds come from?

Sports are not only fun, but *team* sports encourage camaraderie, discipline and commitment—all valuable qualities that compliment a successful life.

It is interesting to note that the slogan, "Life is a team sport," was developed to honor the Hendrick Motorsports NASCAR team members who were killed in a plane crash in October 2004.

As time moved on, I realized that staying fit and healthy necessitated dietary discipline and physical exercise. As life gets busier and busier, it becomes exceedingly more difficult to dedicate time to daily exercise, but, for our bodies, it becomes particularly important. I believe that physical conditioning should be as much a part of our lives as sleeping and eating!

So one of the things I committed to was to stay active ... whatever the cost. My passion for skiing extends back to college days. So, once I moved to Colorado, it made sense to give back to a sport that has provided me with such enjoyment. In the summer of 2008, I trained to become Outdoor Emergency Care (OEC) certified. This certification is equivalent to EMT-Basic and is a requirement of the National Ski Patrol organization. I passed the written test in October 2008, then the practical, on-the-mountain test in mid-December.

Today I participate in the volunteer ski patrol program at the Winter Park ski resort. The 2008/2009 ski season was my first season to volunteer and I look forward to each ski season.

Winter Park also has the nation's leading disabled-skier program ... so plan to see me there, in my wheelchair if necessary ... when I'm 95!

Remember that a healthy body breeds a healthy mind, and success thrives within a healthy mind. Along the way, remind yourself that the path to success and happiness is a journey. Give yourself the tools to travel down that road ... in a balanced way. Too many of us (Yes, I've been a guilty party.) take the trash compactor approach—packing it all in with limited recognizable outcomes.

Choose the things you have a true passion for. Superwoman, the one who attempts to do it all, has, in my opinion, gone the way of the manual typewriter. Balance ... remember it ... balance.

Imagination—Remember to Dream

Early in my life, my dreams were, for the most part, limited by my circumstances and lack of knowledge.

They got bigger with each small success. In a commencement speech to Wellesley College in 1997, Oprah Winfrey related the following story of what she did in celebration of women's dreams:

I asked women to write me their wildest dreams [in celebration of Tina Turner's Wildest Dreams Tour] and tell me what their wildest dreams were. Our intention was to fulfill their wildest dreams. We got

77,000 letters ... 77,000. To our disappointment, we found that the deeper the wound, the smaller the dreams. So many women had such small visions, such small dreams for their lives that we had a difficult time coming up with dreams to fulfill. We did fulfill some. We paid off all the college debt for a young woman whose mother had died, and she put her sisters and brothers through school. We paid off all the bills for a woman who had been battered and managed to put herself and her daughter through college. We sent a woman to Egypt who was dying of cancer, and her lifetime dream was to sit on a camel and use a cell phone. We bought a house for another woman whose dream had always been to have her own home, but because she was battered and had to flee with her children one night, she eventually had to leave the home. And then we fulfilled the dreams women who just wanted to see Oprah ... and meet Tina.

Those were their dreams!

After the gifts were offered some women came crying to me saying, "We didn't know, we didn't know, and this is unfair." I said, That is the lesson: You needed to dream a bigger dream for yourself. That is the lesson.

Even as a young girl I had been fascinated by
far-away places ... like Oklahoma and Arkansas.

Over the years I've been blessed with the
opportunity to travel. A few years ago when
my business took me to Europe for two years,
I had the opportunity to travel even more.
But I had a dream. I wanted to take time away
from work and travel ... really travel ...
to MORE far-away places!

In September 2000, I fulfilled that dream.
I quit my job, put everything I owned in
storage and traveled the world for a year.
My hard work had paid off.

It felt good to be jobless ... and homeless.
Had I been speaking last year [2001], imagine
my introduction, "Welcome our speaker ...
she is jobless ... and homeless!

It was with a great deal of insight that Mark Twain observed, "Travel is fatal to prejudice, bigotry and narrow-mindedness." The more we learn about and experience other cultures and people, the more tolerant and understanding we become; the more balanced our perspectives on life become.

Traveling ... Without Borders

We Americans live in the most prosperous nation on Earth and we tend to believe the rest of the world thinks like us, wants to live like us, wants to eat at McDonalds and drink coffee at Starbucks. In fact, many areas of the world actually make a concerted effort to preserve their culture, disdaining things that are "Americanized" or "Westernized." When I lived in Germany, I noted that McDonalds was humorously referred to as "the American Embassy."

There is no true substitute for experiencing another country and culture first-hand. Somewhere along the way, I stopped being a tourist and became a traveler. The difference? An unattributed quote that has stuck; "A traveler sees what she sees; a tourist sees what she came to see."

Travel is my one true love. He never disappoints me, he gifts me with fascinating friends, he rewards me with a host of incredible life experiences and he embraces me in a warm cloak of happiness.

I recognize that borderless travel isn't for everyone. Economics and logistics, such as family and jobs, limit one's ability to take full advantage of many opportunities. In today's environment, war, terrorism and the fear of traveling outside America's safe-haven is very real.

> *Certainly, travel is more than the seeing of sights; it is a change that goes on, deep and permanent, in the ideas of living.*
> **—Mariam Beard (1876-1958)**
> American historian, author and women's suffrage activist

However, I offer this challenge: Seize every opportunity, however short in duration; take advantage of every occasion, real or virtual, to experience the world and broaden your perspectives.

I have always envisioned my tombstone saying something like, "She tripped on her shoelace and fell off the mountain while trekking in Nepal." Much more interesting and exciting than someone saying, "She was hit by a Denver metro bus."

To tell the truth, quitting my job to travel sounds more cavalier than I felt at the time. I fretted that when I came back to seek employment, prospective employers would view me as a flake.

I sought the advice of a dear friend, Don Walsh, who had interviewed and hired many people in his career at KPMG, the accounting firm where I began my CPA career. I asked Don, "What would you think of someone interviewing for a job in your firm who had a gap in their resumé because they took time to frolic around the world?"

He said two things so important that I wrote them down: "First of all, I view what you're about to do as entrepreneurial. It shows me that you're confident and not afraid to take risks. Why would I not want someone like that working for me? Further, if an employer has a problem with you taking time off in your life, do you want to work for that person anyway?"

I would have most likely taken my sabbatical anyway, but now I could take off with a newfound confidence and peace of mind.

When I began interviewing upon my return from my travels, not only did hiring managers not have an issue with my time off, many were more interested in hearing about my adventures than my work experience!

To fill the gap on my resume, I actually wrote "personal sabbatical" along with the names of the countries in which I traveled. Perhaps I should have taken more time off and traveled to even more places!

Twenty years from now, you will be more disappointed by the things that you didn't do than by the ones you did do. So throw off the bowlines. Sail away from the safe harbor. Catch the trade winds in your sails. Explore. Dream. Discover.
—Mark Twain (1835-1920)
American author and humorist

Even now, hiring managers reviewing my resumé frequently comment that my "personal sabbatical" sets my resumé apart from many other candidates. It shows ingenuity and a take-charge character. Almost every hiring manager begins an interview with, "Tell me more about your sabbatical!"

My friend Don, whose advice proved so valuable, regrettably passed away in December 2008. I so hated that I never had the chance to tell him this story. He loved to be right, and would have proclaimed: TERRIFIC! It was his favorite word.

So what did I do for a whole year? I trekked in
the Himalayan mountains of Nepal and
Tibet; climbed Mt.Kilimanjaro in Tanzania,
Africa, followed by a safari on the wild plains
of the Serengeti; bicycled through Vietnam;
backpacked through Cambodia and Thailand,
feasting on their rich cuisines; enjoyed a variety
of activities in Australia (biking, hiking, sailing,
river-rafting and scuba-diving)—held a koala
in my arms and fed kangaroos; trekked up a
tepuy (flat-topped mountain) in Venezuela.
I thanked God for American democracy as I
barely escaped a political uprising over upcoming
government elections that left 35 people dead on
the island of Zanzibar off the eastern coast of
Tanzania, Africa. And I woke up every single
morning feeling incredibly blessed that I had this
amazing opportunity to experience the rich
cultures and people of other nations, to behold
the magnificent splendor of the Himalayan
mountains, to touch the red soil of the Australian
Outback, to watch the wild lions, elephants and
kangaroos run free in their natural habitat.

At the same time, I felt extraordinarily thankful
that I would be going home to a country where
one's limitations are measured only in one's
own mind. Where it's possible for a young

country girl from East Texas to make her way to an 18,000-foot mountain vista in Nepal, to gaze upon the highest point on Earth: Mt. Everest.

Traveling with no time limitations or hard and fast schedule allowed me to truly experience the places I visited. I began my sabbatical visiting friends in Europe; then I chose destinations that would not be on my radar for normal vacation time: Nepal, Tibet, Tanzania in eastern Africa, Zanzibar, Australia, Tasmania, Vietnam, Cambodia, Thailand, and Venezuela, with short stop-offs in South Korea and India.

Home Sweet Home

Not every place I traveled was a "vacation" by most people's definition. Even in Nepal, which I consider one of my favorite destinations, the political unrest, impoverished populace, human suffering and the constant uncertainty of life were eye-opening. Narrowly escaping the political riots in Zanzibar was frightening. I vowed to never complain about the United States again!

I am frequently asked whether I traveled ALONE. The answer is yes—and no. Yes, I was alone, but on certain excursions, arranged through an adventure travel company (for example, the month-long trek through the Nepal Himalayan Mountains), I traveled with a group. Traveling alone gave me the flexibility to make unplanned detours, stay longer in places that interested me and meet people more easily. THAT was the beauty of my travels, affording me the most incredible experience of my life.

One's destination is never a place, but a new way of seeing things.

—Henry Miller (1891-1980)
American novelist and painter

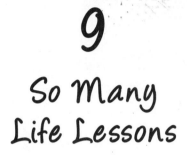

9

So Many
Life Lessons

Instructions for living a life:
Pay attention.
Be astonished.
Tell about it.

— Mary Oliver
American Poet

Duuring my rocky but adventurous travels through life, I learned a number of important things about relationships and marriage:

- The art of compromise heads the list. John Gray wrote *Men are from Mars and Women are from Venus*. What he is saying is that each gender processes information differently. In most instances, the only gateway to peace is through compromise.

  It is often the little things that, over time, disintegrate relationships. Do you argue over whether the toilet tissue should roll over the top or under? Does it really matter? Do you disagree on the little things ... the big things?

  Why not agree to disagree? By agreeing to do this, little things won't become an issue.

  It worked for me. It was the toilet tissue that got us in the end—just kidding.
- Trust and Respect are high on the list. Both are so intertwined with love that the loss of either is generally fatal to the relationship ... which is based on love.

- There are many things that I have learned from and through my friends; their lives and choices. I chose to not have children, but I recognize that the decision to have them should and must be mutual—both parties should want to bring little ones into the world. In addition, children deserve to be wanted and not be the product of someone else's desires or expectations.

- I learned that there is a difference between the two "L" words: love and lust. Sometimes it is difficult to distinguish between the two, but I learned that lust diminishes over time, and love survives, and even grows, through experiences and time. Lust has a way of camouflaging future issues and clouding one's judgment.

- Although difficult, I've come to understand that it is imperative to ask a lot of questions before diving into "marriage"—not only questions that I ask my future partner, but the hard ones I should be asking of myself. A variety of topics need to be considered: children, career goals, religious affiliations, hobbies, and passions.

- Finding fault with a partner is an easy trap to slide into ... blaming one another and keeping score. What purpose does either serve? Both are highly damaging to the relationship, and to oneself.
- Experience has taught me that disagreements are inevitable ... and quite normal. However, it is best to resolve the issues before both parties go to bed ... angry.
- One must love themselves before they can truly fall in love. This is a universal principal ... we cannot give what we don't have. Make loving yourself a priority and watch what happens.
- No one can make you happy. In the movie "Jerry McGuire," Tom Cruise's character found someone to "complete" him. But, completion must first come from within. I learned that I have to be a complete person on my own first.
- Romance often fades in marriage, and romantic movies are just that—romantic movies ... entertaining works of fiction.
- Relationships take a significant amount of commitment. If we're not ready, we should, as

difficult as it might be, save ourselves and others a lot of heartache and move on.

- All relationships demand a certain amount of time and a great deal of attention. Prioritizing my life in order to fulfill those commitments is essential if I want my relationships to work ... and grow.

- Relationships are fluid ... they change over time. I learned that I need to be more flexible, adaptable and aware of the many dynamics that come into play when merging my life, in any capacity, with another's.

- The phrase "happily ever after" is one of fairy tales. This was a hard one to swallow because my generation grew up believing in the Cinderella Syndrome. However, a successful partnering just doesn't magically happen; it requires dedication and nurturing. Romantic movies and books may perpetrate the happily-ever-after myth, but it is a product of Hollywood...not real life.

- When we fail to accept someone for who they are—with all their faults and failings—we are doing them, and ourselves, a disservice. Loving unconditionally is tough. Eventually, it seems, we want to change our love

interests ... make them better. If we accept
that no one is perfect, not even ourselves,
we begin to relax and love unconditionally.

- Forgiveness is an art; it is the underlying
  foundation for peace of mind and happiness.
  Practicing forgiveness does not mean,
  however, that we should sacrifice our integrity
  and values. Sometimes we might forgive, but
  then move on. Forgive, don't condone.
- In order to have a quality relationship,
  focused time with my partner, must be
  a priority. In my quest for professional
  success, early on, I didn't recognize the
  significance of this fundamental rule and I
  paid the price.
- Each must maintain their own identity within
  a partnership. Getting lost in one another
  does just that—gets you both lost.
- When love isn't returned ... move on. Life
  doesn't stop and hearts don't break (although
  it feels like they do). Allow yourself time to
  grieve, then get on with the business of living.
  Years ago as I mourned an unrequited love
  interest, a wise friend said to me, "You're
  allowing this person to occupy your heart ...
  rent-free. Evict him." I did.

- Laughter is cathartic. And, in a relationship, profoundly vital. No matter how difficult things get, keep in mind that laughter soothes the soul—even if it means laughing at yourself.

You don't stop laughing because you grow old. You grow old because you stop laughing.
—Michael Pritchard
Keynote speaker—PBS educational videos

- Marriage is not a prerequisite to a happy fulfilled life. It is infinitely better to be happily single than unhappily married. Sometimes we let the expectations and values of friends, family or society override our own judgment ... tread wisely as it is YOUR life you need to be living.

  Katherine Hepburn, the outspoken actress, once said, "If you want to sacrifice the admiration of many men for the criticism of one, go ahead and get married."
- And lastly, never give up on love. Again, borrowing from Winston Churchill, "Never give up, never, never, never!"

10

From Simms to Zanzibar— What the Heck Does That Mean?

Leave the comfort of the beaten path and
blaze a trail into the wildemess.
You just might discover something extraordinary.
That something may be You.

—lynn

When people read a book, they expect to find the title explained or at least restated within its pages.

You are probably clear how Simms came into the picture, but you are probably wondering about Zanzibar. In addition, you'd probably like to know what relationship the book's title has to success, Simms ... and me!

Actually, Simms and Zanzibar are both geographic locations, half a world apart.

Simms—Located within the Republic of Texas

Simms is a small town in the far northeast corner of the Republic of Texas. (Sorry, I'm a loyal Texan.)

Zanzibar is an island off the eastern coast of Africa, part of the Republic of Tanzania. They have absolutely nothing in common other than the fact that they both have played a considerable role in my life.

Although I've talked about Simms already, allow me to continue to paint a picture of the place where I went to high school.

Imagine yourself driving the back roads of Bowie County Texas in 1971. As you approach the intersection of Highway 67 and Highway 98, you see a blinking traffic signal, a combination general store and post office, and the First Baptist Church of Simms. Fuel at the general store is 30 cents a gallon. The road sign indicates that you have entered the unincorporated community of Simms—population 230.

Along the highways, you see a handful of houses, from turn-of-the-century frame farmhouses with steep pitched roofs, to the more recent and modest, brick homes. They sit far from the roads and are tucked in amongst scores of pine, oak, magnolia, pecan and sweet gum trees that dominate the scene. Your eyes are then drawn to the large, multicolored stone building that is James Bowie School, built in 1936, and named after the hero of the Alamo.

According to the Handbook of Texas Online, the community was named for G.W. Simms, who played a major role in securing a post office for the area in 1890.

James Bowie High School in 1961, as it also appeared in 1971.

The gym before it burned.

In 1892 Simms had a gristmill, a gin, a store and a population of about 50. By 1914 the population had grown to 150. It slid back to a low of 50 in the '30s and began to grow again in the '40s. In1982 Simms had a population of 240 and a whopping four businesses. The population through 2000 was still reported at 240—too distant from any large city to benefit from the population explosion of the '80s and '90s.

If you drive through Simms today, you will see that it boasts a modern post office, and general store that burned to the ground in the spring of 2009, but has since been rebuilt.

The town's gasoline prices have risen tenfold since 1971; the trees, which are much larger now, obscure the view of the school.

The First Baptist Church has a different pastor, the solitary traffic light still blinks uninterrupted and the high school still sports the Pirate as its mascot. The population remains at several hundred.

Zanzibar—A Stop-Off Half a World Away

Zanzibar, on the other hand, is a place that is the polar opposite of Simms. The province is made up of numerous small islands off the coast of eastern Africa. The largest island, Ungula, is the one known as "Zanzibar," and became part of the Republic of Tanzania in 1964.

Zanzibar was founded over ten centuries ago by Arabs who used its natural harbor as a hub for the slave, ivory, clove and spice trades.

Today it is a predominately Sunni Moslem society that has a population of over one million. Its claim to pop-culture fame is that it is the birthplace of Freddie Mercury, founder of the rock band "Queen."

The first four months of my sabbatical were spent trekking in Nepal, Tibet and on Mt. Kilimanjaro in Tanzania. After my trek up Mt. Kilimanjaro, I flew to Zanzibar for a much-needed rest and to take time to reflect on my travel experiences ... thus far.

I was traveling with no particular agenda, and I also needed some down-time to decide where to go next.

After trekking up mountains and sleeping in tents, I decided to treat myself in Zanzibar to a hotel room on the beach. Strolling along the beach, absorbing and photographing brilliant sunsets and touring the Old Town of Zanzibar were a pleasant break from my recent physical activities.

Earlier, I mentioned narrowly missing a political uprising. While touring Old Town, I began to notice an unusual amount of graffiti on the ancient walls. Unlike New York City where graffiti is commonplace, this particular collection seemed new and ... incongruous. I asked my guide what it meant, and he said that Zanzibar was on the eve of political elections and the graffiti was the opposing party's way of protesting the incumbent government.

A few days after I departed for Paris, the political riots erupted, killing 35 people, injuring many others and closing down the airport from which I departed.

Meanwhile, on the other side of the world, the United States was experiencing its own version of political rioting called the 2000 Presidential Election.

While trekking in the Himalayan Mountains of Nepal and Tibet, I didn't have many opportunities to follow the United States' presidential election of 2000, but I did, of course, hear about the embarrassing debacle; faulty punch card ballots and missing names on the voting rolls in Florida which necessitated an historic review and subsequent ruling by the U.S. Supreme court to halt a recount in the state. That process resulted in a victory for George W. Bush.

I was frequently asked, as the token American in most situations, to explain the American presidential election process and the reason for the calamity. My American Government class was too far in the past to remember the specific ins and outs of the Electoral College, but even so, the 2000 election fiasco was not easily explained either.

American democracy ultimately prevailed, and the new American president was declared. I watched the inauguration of President Bush from a beach bar in Zanzibar, enjoying the beautiful sunset over the Indian Ocean. The ignominy of U.S. politics was too far removed to disrupt the peace and serenity I was enjoying in Zanzibar.

Why Zanzibar? What It Meant to Me

When I wasn't touring the Old Town of Zanzibar, photographing sunsets or watching the presidential inauguration, I was digesting my experiences. The Zanzibar beach was a perfect place to take a deep breath and think about the people and places I had encountered.

I expected to be reminiscing about my extraordinary view of Mt. Everest (29,029 feet above sea level), while standing at 18,000 feet … or the stunning photo I took of the Dalai Lama's winter palace in Lhasa, Tibet … or the wild African plains of the Serengeti in the shadow of Mt. Kilimanjaro.

Instead, I found myself remembering the school children in Nepal asking for pencils as our group walked through their schoolyard. I could not erase from my mind the smiles of the Tibetan children as we washed the thick layer of grime off their faces and dried blood from their infected ears (from being pierced for earrings). Or, the Tanzanian boy who asked me to send him an English book when I got home so he could learn our language. And disturbingly, my mind kept returning to the graffiti on the Old Town walls.

A heavy hand of sadness lay on my shoulders. I saw all the luxuries of life I took for granted flash before me. My grandfather's old house was transformed into a mansion. The outhouse suddenly looked very sanitary. The well water was clean and available. I had more pencils, pens and paper than I would ever need. My school had a library full of books.

My journey had come full circle on that Zanzibar beach. I would forever see, experience and appreciate life in a whole new way.

That was my epiphany. And that is why Zanzibar became part of my book's title.

Gratitude bestows reverence, allowing us to encounter everyday epiphanies, those transcendent moments of awe that change forever how we experience life and the world.

—John Milton
English poet, historian and scholar

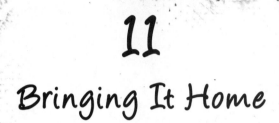

11
Bringing It Home

*A graduation ceremony is an event
where the commencement speaker tells
thousands of students dressed in identical
caps and gowns that individuality is
the key to success.*

—Bob Orben
*American magician and
professional comedy writer*

The word 'commencement' means "a new start" or "beginning". When you leave here tonight, each of you will have your own trail to blaze. I hope a small portion of my journey will give you some ideas or guide posts for your journey. Now, it is up to YOU to create your own destiny.

Congratulations Class of 2002!

Thank you all and God Bless!

 *I hate quotations. Tell me what you know.*

—**Ralph Waldo Emerson**

12

Lynn's Notes

(Way more interesting
than CliffsNotes™)

I n closing, I would like to share a few more tidbits I've learned from my journeys.

Be yourself—everyone else is taken. (Taken from a sign at a ski lodge ... I thought it was profound.)

Enjoy your youth. It only happens once!

Laugh a lot. Laughter is infectious; it is one of the best natural, organic, gut-level medicines. In my opinion ... a day without laughter is like a ski day without snow.

Celebrate successes. Every success, no matter how small, is worth celebrating.

Radiate enthusiasm. Enthusiasm is contagious. It is an active energy that has the power to transform how people view you. Enthusiasm is the fuel to success's fire.

Be on time. Too few people pay attention to this very simple courtesy. It makes a huge difference in how people view you ... it is an aspect of your integrity.

Keep a journal. Not only is it a record of your life, but writing it can be cathartic. Your journal could simply chronicle your family history or become your future book. (Did you really think I remembered all the events I talked about in this book?)

Write a book. Why not? Sam Horn, author and speaker, said, "I've never met an author that was sorry they wrote a book; they are only sorry they did not write it sooner." I concur.

Be a source of inspiration, not consternation. (Parents and teachers love that small piece of advice.)

Mean what you say. If you say you'll call—call.

Approach marriage with careful reflection. After "preaching" about the importance of family, this is not to discourage the institution, only to highlight the fact that marriage is hard work ... approach it with your eyes open.

Respect children. Allow me to remind you of my recollection of the conversation with my Mother at the age of four. It obviously had a significant impact on me since I remembered it so many years later!

Learn how to spell and pronounce the two "H" words—Humility and Humbleness. More importantly, practice them. No job, no chore, no random act of kindness should be beneath you.

Get off the Internet and read a book. I've never met a successful person that is not an avid reader. Reading is relaxing, good therapy, intellectually stimulating and a cure for insomnia (sometimes ...)

Be financially responsible. Pay attention to things like your credit report. Pay bills on time. Simple things reap huge benefits.

Live up to your commitments. Be a person of your word; your success depends on it. Would you continue doing business with a car repair shop that commits to have your car ready in one day and it always takes three or four? Consider the employee who commits to completing assignments and continually fails to meet their deadlines? Think about a friend who commits to feeding your dog while you're on vacation and just doesn't get around to it? Trust is easier to maintain than to rebuild.

Be accountable for your actions. Take responsibility for your decisions ... your life. Avoid blaming things on other people. YOU must decide how you will behave. You are the architect of your life. Nobody owns you. Once an adult, no one can make you do something you don't want to do. Remember your parents' lease is typically up when you turn eighteen or graduate from college.

Never allow convention to stymie your growth. Think outside the box. Don't do things just because everyone else does—and don't NOT do things just because everyone else doesn't.

R.S.V.P. This is a simple act that's not much trouble yet, it is highly valued. When you're invited to a party or event, take the time to RESPOND!

Send thank-you notes. It sounds silly, but once you've actually attended a function, sending a thank-you note to the host means a lot.

Don't be a bridge burner. The big world is a relatively small place. We might daydream about telling off our bosses, telling them what you really think of them, throwing your office keys on their desks or telling them where to stuff it, but then what happens? What if the new company you hired into is acquired by your old company and your new boss is ... surprise ... your old boss?

Never hold grudges. Not only is it counter-productive and distracting from life's pleasures, it can be stressful and detrimental to your health. It's easy to hold a grudge, but it takes character to forgive.

Give compliments. Think about how a sincere compliment from someone brightens your day. Brighten someone else's day.

Accept compliments graciously. A simple "thank you" suffices.

Pay it forward. Do someone an unconditional favor.

Choose carefully. The choices you make in life determine the quality of your life, and only YOU are responsible for those choices.

Take chances—just don't stand behind a fly-fisherman. Living cautiously is safe…. Taking chances makes life worthwhile.

*Don't wait for the storm to pass—
learn to ski the powder!*

—lynn

Embrace change. Change is the only real constant in our lives. Success is interwoven with our ability to deal with change.

Protect your integrity. Our integrity, honor and honesty are the things people remember most about their time with us. Although in a constantly shifting world we want to embrace change, be wary of compromising quality, ethics and values. Your reputation, based on integrity, is your most valuable asset.

Make things happen. Mary Kay Ash (founder of Mary Kay Cosmetics) described three types of people in the world: "Those who make things happen; those who watch things happen; and those who wonder what happened." My version of this advice is to ask yourself whether you want to be the driver, the backseat driver or the passive rider.

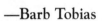

"Be brave. Be willing to go where the common are afraid to go.

—Barb Tobias
author of *Tossed and Found; Where frugal is Chic*

Network. Remember that it is not always *what* you know that will get you ahead … it is more often a case of *who* you know. Aside from my first job out of college, every job I've secured has been a result of *who* I knew. With the downward spiral of the economy, the importance of networking has never been more apparent. And, while *who* you know may open doors, *what* you know will keep you there.

Don't complain—offer solutions. Complaining is easy; identifying solutions requires brain power and introspection.

Don't waste time playing the "regret" game. There will always be things you regret having done, or roads you wish you had never traveled. Don't waste time dwelling on the past or lost opportunities or the poor choices you've made. Someone once said that anyone who says they have no regrets hasn't lived life. Learn from those experiences and move on.

Don't allow your past to define your future. Looking back, I realize that my disruptive family life was not that unusual. Therefore, blaze your own path, create your own norm and be responsible for your own life.

Keep your childlike curiosity. I don't believe curiosity killed the cat—it was the dog.

Avoid gossip. Everyone enjoys a little juicy gossip now and then—read it in the tabloids, don't spread it. Spreading what often turns out to be false stories will, in many cases, destroy your credibility.

Pay attention to your appearance. Adhere to the old saying that you get only one chance to make a good first impression. Like it or not, we are judged by our appearance. Remember the scene in the movie Pretty Woman when Julia Robert's character, Vivian, went shopping in a hooker outfit? No one would wait on her. She went back exquisitely dressed and had salespeople falling all over her.

Be a good listener. You always learn more by listening. People may even think you're a wonderful conversationalist, so don't prove them wrong by talking too much. Turn off cell phones, don't text and give the other party your full attention.

Never allow fear to paralyze you. A few years ago, a skiing accident required me to have knee surgery. To the surprise of my friends, I was skiing again four months later. Two years later, I had another skiing accident and yet another knee surgery—the other knee. Both surgeries required intense rehabilitation. Whenever I was asked if I was now going to give it up, my response was always "Why? If you have a car accident, do you stop driving?"

On occasion, take time to reflect on your life. Ask yourself a question about your journey. If you could go back in time, what advice would you give your younger self? Pay that advice forward.

Perhaps one of the more important pieces of advice I can give is:

Rejoice in life like it was your last day on Earth. Plan for it like you are going to live forever. CARPE DIEM (Seize the Day).

Life is not a journey to the grave with the intent of arriving all pretty and preserved; but rather to skid in broadside thoroughly used up, totally worn out and loudly proclaiming; WOW! WHAT A RIDE!

—lynn's motto, **Author unknown**